THE WHITEBOARD BIBLE®

VOLUME 2

A NATION DIVIDED
to
THE GOSPELS

Allen Jackson

PASTOR, WORLD OUTREACH CHURCH

allenjackson.com

© 2015 by   for The Whiteboard
Bible Vol. 2: A Nation Divided to The
Gospels. First edition 2014. Revised
edition 2015.

The Whiteboard Bible® by Allen
Jackson Ministries

Published by Allen Jackson Ministries
1921 New Salem Road, Hwy. 99
Murfreesboro, TN 37128

Special Sales:
Most Allen Jackson Ministries books
are available at special quantity
discounts when purchased in bulk
by corporations, organizations, and
special-interest groups. Custom
imprinting or excerpting can also be
done to fit special needs. For more
information, please email:
contact@allenjackson.com.

Illustrations: Imago
Design: Tommy Owen

ISBN: 978-1-61718-028-6

THE WHITEBOARD BIBLE®

A NATION DIVIDED *to* THE GOSPELS

CONTENTS

APPENDIX

SMALL GROUP LEADERS

ABOUT THE AUTHOR

INTRODUCTION

The Bible is a collection of sixty-six books. Many different authors contributed to the work. It was written in different cultural settings over a period of hundreds of years. The books are not arranged in chronological order. The names seem unusual, and the places are mostly unknown. It is not surprising that most Christians do not understand the Bible. We typically settle for a verse that offers comfort or hope and imagine that in a handful of verses we have the essence of this remarkable book.

The Bible tells a story. The amazing narrative begins with creation and concludes with Jesus triumphant. Between Genesis and Revelation is the story of God's interaction with the descendants of Adam. The Bible is not intended to be a science book or a history book. It is possible to gain historical insight from reading the Bible and even to understand our world better. The primary objective is to provide the reader insight into Almighty God and His interactions with the descendants of Adam.

Often, we avoid reading the Bible thinking it is simply too complex or boring. The Whiteboard Study has been designed to help anyone gain a fundamental understanding of the narrative of the Bible. Inside the books of the Bible are amazing accounts of men and women whose lives were transformed by God. The Bible unfolds a revelation of God that invites all readers toward hope and purpose.

Through three volumes we will develop a twelve-point timeline that will serve as the framework for all the characters and events in the Bible. We will take a journey from creation through the emergence of the Hebrew people. We will hear the prophets and listen to the Sadducees challenge Jesus. By the time the Whiteboard Study is complete we will be able to recount the progression of the biblical events in a simple, sequential order.

This second volume begins with a civil war in Israel and continues through the Gospels. We will review an often overlooked part of Israelite history. After Solomon died the nation of Israel was torn apart. The Promised Land was occupied by two nations, Judah and Israel. The hearts of the people had turned away from God, and He sent judgment in the form of conquering armies. The exile is one of the most challenging periods of Jewish history. The faithfulness of God is demonstrated powerfully in the return of the exiles and the building of the second temple. Jesus stepped into the story at this point. The Gospels are not a new a story but a very important chapter of the story that was begun in Genesis. A God of mercy intervened to provide redemption for those who will accept Him.

The Bible is not beyond knowing. If you will invest as little as ten minutes a day in reading through your Bible, in the course of one year you can read through this amazing book. The expression of this small discipline can change your life.

Allen Jackson

OUTLINE OF EACH SESSION

A typical group session for *The Whiteboard Bible* will include the following:

GETTING STARTED. The foundation for spiritual growth is an intimate connection with God and His family. A few people who really know you and who earn your trust provide a place to experience the life Jesus invites you to live. Using the icebreaker questions enables you to connect with one or two in your group to begin the discussion with ease.

DVD TEACHING SEGMENT. Serving as a companion to *The Whiteboard Bible* small group study guide is *The Whiteboard Bible* video teaching. This DVD is designed to present unique illustrations from the whiteboard and helpful teaching segments from Pastor Allen Jackson.

DISCUSSION. This section is where you will process as a group the teaching from the DVD. We want to help you apply the insights from Scripture practically, creatively, and from your heart as well as your head. Allowing the timeless truths from God's Word to transform our lives in Christ is our greatest aim.

APPLICATION. The objective of Bible study is not primarily information but transformation. Each week we will walk through questions intended to help us not only to learn but to apply what we have learned to our daily life.

DEEPER BIBLE STUDY. If you have time and want to dig deeper into more Bible passages about the topic at hand, we've provided additional passages and questions. Your group may choose to do homework after of each meeting in order to cover more biblical material. If you prefer not to do homework, the Going Deeper section will provide you with plenty to discuss within the group. These options allow individuals or the whole group to expand their study, while still accommodating those who can't do homework or are new to your group.

DAILY DEVOTIONALS. Each week on the Daily Devotionals pages we provide Scriptures to read and reflect on between group meetings. We suggest you use this section to seek God on your own throughout the week. This time at home should begin and end with prayer. Don't get in a hurry; take enough time to hear God's direction.

WEEKLY MEMORY VERSES. For each session we have provided a Memory Verse that emphasizes an important truth from the session. Memorizing Scripture can be a vital part of filling our minds with God's will for our lives. We encourage you to give this important habit a try.

READ ALOUD. Inside the Application and Discussion sections are additional teaching components to use with your group. These sections are a natural way to set up more dialogue for the questions that follow and also serve as a great tool for opening discussion in your group.

WEEK 1

INTRODUCTION

Welcome to *The Whiteboard Bible*, a way of learning God's Word that enables us to understand the story of the Bible and not just a collection of Bible stories. As we begin volume two, we step into the heart of the Hebrew Bible. The Israelites are at home in the Promised Land. The monarchy has been firmly established, but the warnings of the prophets remind the people that each generation must choose to honor God. These six sessions will guide you through a tumultuous time in Israelite history. Take a

A NATION DIVIDED

little time each week to review the timeline. The points along this chronological map will help you to organize the familiar names and events in a sequential order. The powerful drama of God and people will emerge in a more personal way as the Bible becomes a coherent series of events and not just a collection of random events and mystical figures from the past. Almighty God has a purpose for each life. Recognizing the epic panorama of Scripture will add momentum to our individual journeys.

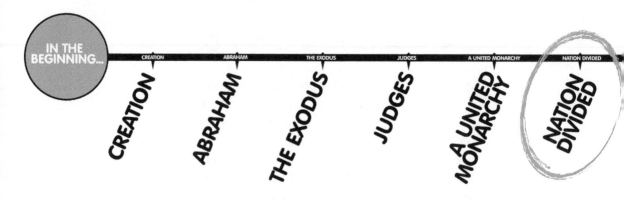

IN THE BEGINNING...

CREATION   ABRAHAM   THE EXODUS   JUDGES   A UNITED MONARCHY   NATION DIVIDED

CREATION

ABRAHAM

THE EXODUS

JUDGES

A UNITED MONARCHY

NATION DIVIDED

THE **WHITEBOARD** BIBLE

GETTING STARTED

Begin the session with a question below or brief activity to become better acquainted with one another. Then take a minute to introduce yourself to those in the group.

1 Which biblical character other than Jesus would you most like to meet, and why?

2 Which book in the Bible is hardest for you to understand?

THE PROPHETS · EXILE · THE SECOND TEMPLE · THE GOSPELS · THE CHURCH · JESUS' RETURN · **ONWARD!**

THE PROPHETS

EXILE

THE SECOND TEMPLE

THE GOSPELS

THE CHURCH

JESUS' RETURN

OUTLINE OF DVD LESSON
Use the outline below to follow along during the DVD.

I. Peer Pressure

1 Samuel 8:19-20
[19] But the people refused to listen to Samuel. "No!" they said. "We want a king over us. [20] Then we will be like all the other nations, with a king to lead us and to go out before us and fight our battles."

A. Syncretism

B. Expressions of Grace
1. Judges
2. Kings
3. Limits of grace

II. The History Books

A. Nation Divided
1. Israel (Northern Kingdom)—Samaria, King Jereboam
2. Judah (Southern Kingdom)—Jerusalem, King Rehoboam

B. Two Stories Told in Parallel
1 Kings 15:9-10
[9] In the twentieth year of Jeroboam king of Israel, Asa became king of Judah, [10] and he reigned in Jerusalem forty-one years.

C. Rebellion
1. Ungodly Momentum

"Rebellion was not just against a young king, it was against God—it unleashed consequences which were unwanted momentum away from God."

2. Power of God's People

1 Kings 18:20-21
[20] *So Ahab sent word throughout all Israel and assembled the prophets on Mount Carmel.* [21] *Elijah went before the people and said, "How long will you waver between two opinions? If the LORD is God, follow him; but if Baal is God, follow him." But the people said nothing.*

2 Chronicles 7:13-14
[13] *"When I shut up the heavens so that there is no rain, or command locusts to devour the land or send a plague among my people,* [14] *if my people, who are called by my name, will humble themselves and pray and seek my face and turn from their wicked ways, then will I hear from heaven and will forgive their sin and will heal their land."*

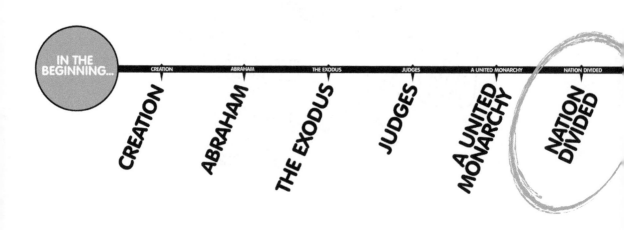

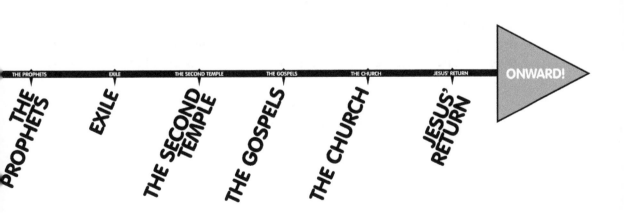

THE PROPHETS   EXILE   THE SECOND TEMPLE   THE GOSPELS   THE CHURCH   JESUS' RETURN

DISCUSSION

Using the questions that follow, we will review and expand on the teaching we just experienced.

1 Who was the last of Israel's judges?

1 Samuel 8:4-7

⁴ *So all the elders of Israel gathered together and came to Samuel at Ramah.* ⁵ *They said to him, "You are old, and your sons do not walk in your ways; now appoint a king to lead us, such as all the other nations have."* ⁶ *But when they said, "Give us a king to lead us," this displeased Samuel; so he prayed to the* Lord. ⁷ *And the* Lord *told him: "Listen to all that the people are saying to you; it is not you they have rejected, but they have rejected me as their king."*

2 What three reasons did the Israelite leaders offer to support their request for a king?

READ ALOUD

Samuel is a very important figure in the biblical narrative. His leadership provided a transition from the judges to the monarchy. Samuel had to overcome personal rejection and respond to the tribal leaders with compassion. His remarkable character enabled him to anoint the first two kings of Israel. Even after the establishment of the monarchy, Samuel was a powerful figure in Israelite life. Saul sought his blessing and even went to a medium to contact Samuel after his death.

3 Samuel was being replaced as leader, but God said it was not Samuel who was being rejected. In reality, who were the Israelites rejecting?

4 God directed Samuel to anoint the first two kings of Israel. Who were they?

5 Solomon was the last king to reign over a united nation. What are the names of the two nations that emerged and what were their capital cities?

6 What city was the location of Solomon's temple?

7 What challenges would the absence of the temple in the Northern Kingdom (Israel) create?

APPLICATION

Now it's time to make some personal applications of all we've been thinking about in the last few minutes.

READ ALOUD

Grace and rebellion—for hundreds of years God expressed grace and forgiveness toward Israel. Yet rebellion was a recurring problem. God would provide leaders, deliverance, and victories over enemies and even select a king. The tendency to reject God's way and choose their own persisted.

> **1 Kings 12:26-30**
>
> *26 Jeroboam thought to himself, "The kingdom will now likely revert to the house of David. 27 If these people go up to offer sacrifices at the temple of the LORD in Jerusalem, they will again give their allegiance to their lord, Rehoboam king of Judah. They will kill me and return to King Rehoboam." 28 After seeking advice, the king made two golden calves. He said to the people, "It is too much for you to go up to Jerusalem. Here are your gods, O Israel, who brought you up out of Egypt." 29 One he set up in Bethel, and the other in Dan. 30 And this thing became a sin; the people went even as far as Dan to worship the one there.*

8 What was Jeroboam's motivation for installing golden calves?

9 There always seem to be reasons to choose ungodliness. What are contemporary examples of this type of dilemma?

God sent the prophets to remind the people of God's point of view. Sometimes they would repent, and sometimes they would stubbornly continue apart from God. It is helpful to recognize the personal requirements for cooperating with God. Throughout the ages, some people cooperate with God while others face the same opportunities and choose to go their own way. We should not anticipate universal acceptance of God's invitations. Rather, we must choose to honor God for ourselves and encourage others to do the same.

1 Kings 16:31-33

³¹ He not only considered it trivial to commit the sins of Jeroboam son of Nebat, but he also married Jezebel daughter of Ethbaal king of the Sidonians, and began to serve Baal and worship him. ³² He set up an altar for Baal in the temple of Baal that he built in Samaria. ³³ Ahab also made an Asherah pole and did more to provoke the LORD, the God of Israel, to anger than did all the kings of Israel before him.

10 Who was King Ahab's wife? What was her nationality?

11 Focusing attention on foreign gods diminished the influence of Jerusalem. A politically expedient decision encouraged rebellion. Identify politically or financially expedient choices that can promote ungodliness.

2 Chronicles 7:13-14

¹³ "When I shut up the heavens so that there is no rain, or command locusts to devour the land or send a plague among my people, ¹⁴ if my people, who are called by my name, will humble themselves and pray and seek my face and turn from their wicked ways, then will I hear from heaven and will forgive their sin and will heal their land."

12 The power of repentance rests with God's people. List the four things God requires of His people to enlist His support.

13 Rebellion and repentance are a repetitive cycle in Scripture. Describe a time in your life you chose rebellion. Describe a time of repentance.

14 Discuss ways you can utilize your influence in a "prophetic manner," encouraging people to embrace a God-perspective.

READ ALOUD

God's people are the difference-makers in the unfolding story of history. Just as certainly as God called Samuel, David, or Esther, He has prepared people for this generation. The challenge is not the depth of the darkness but the willingness of those who hold the light to stand up.

15 As you conclude, list three or four ways contemporary faith is under pressure to "be like all the other nations" and discuss what a God-honoring decision would be. (Ask the Holy Spirit to help you!)

PRAYER

Close the session in prayer. Share prayer requests with the group, and pray for each other. Close by praying the following prayer together.

Heavenly Father, I acknowledge You as the source of my life. Thank You for Your extravagant provision on my behalf. I choose to walk in Your path. May Your abiding presence bring distinction to my life. I repent of all compromise and rebellious attitudes. I want to cooperate fully with You. May Your people humble themselves before You and seek Your face that healing may come to our land. In Jesus' name, amen.

Prayer requests this week:

GOING DEEPER

This section is designed to do as homework, if you choose, between your Small Group meetings.

....

Who are you listening to? King Rehoboam sought counsel.

1 Kings 12:3-16

³ So they sent for Jeroboam, and he and the whole assembly of Israel went to Rehoboam and said to him: ⁴ "Your father put a heavy yoke on us, but now lighten the harsh labor and the heavy yoke he put on us, and we will serve you." ⁵ Rehoboam answered, "Go away for three days and then come back to me." So the people went away. ⁶ Then King Rehoboam consulted the elders who had served his father Solomon during his lifetime. "How would you advise me to answer these people?" he asked. ⁷ They replied, "If today you will be a servant to these people and serve them and give them a favorable answer, they will always be your servants." ⁸ But Rehoboam rejected the advice the elders gave him and consulted the young men who had grown up with him and were serving him. ⁹ He asked them, "What is your advice? How should we answer these people who say to me, 'Lighten the yoke your father put on us'?" ¹⁰ The young men who had grown up with him replied, "Tell these people who have said to you, 'Your father put a heavy yoke on us, but make our yoke lighter'—tell them, 'My little finger is thicker than my father's waist. ¹¹ My father laid on you a heavy yoke; I will make it even heavier. My father scourged you with whips; I will scourge you with scorpions.'" ¹² Three days later Jeroboam and all the people returned to Rehoboam, as the king had said, "Come back to me in three days." ¹³ The king answered the people harshly. Rejecting the advice given him by the elders, ¹⁴ he followed the advice of the young men and said, "My father made your yoke heavy; I will make it even heavier. My father scourged you with whips; I will scourge you with scorpions." ¹⁵ So the king did not listen to the people, for this turn of events was from the LORD, to fulfill the word the LORD had spoken to Jeroboam son of Nebat through Ahijah the Shilonite. ¹⁶ When all Israel saw that the king refused to listen to them, they answered the king: "What share do we have in David, what part in Jesse's son? To your tents, O Israel! Look after your own house, O David!" So the Israelites went home.

After the death of King Solomon, his son Rehoboam was assumed to be king. Solomon was a great king, but he had treated the people harshly in his old age (as Samuel had warned). The people of Israel desired a reprieve from the burden of the forced labor and heavy taxation of Solomon's reign. If Rehoboam would agree to lighten the load, Israel promised their allegiance.

- What were the first steps Rehoboam took in receiving counsel to make decisions in the way he would rule?

- Were his beginning steps to finding wise counsel good ones?

- Why did Rehoboam seek further counsel of his peers beyond that of his elders?

- What was the outcome of his decision?

Psalm 25:1, 4-5
Prayer of King David
1 In you I trust, O my God. 4 Show me your ways, O Lord, teach me your paths;
5 guide me in your truth and teach me, for you are God my Savior, and my hope is in you all day long.

- What could Rehoboam have learned from his grandfather David?

- Are you currently in a season in which you need to make an important decision? How can you learn from Rehoboam's experience?

DAILY REFLECTIONS

These are daily reviews of the key Bible verses and related others that will help you think about and apply the insights from this session.

DAY 1

Psalm 51:1-2

God's Mercy

¹ Have mercy on me, O God, according to your unfailing love; according to your great compassion blot out my transgressions. ² Wash away all my iniquity and cleanse me from my sin.

Reflection Question:
Why is God's mercy and unfailing love in our lives so important? How have you experienced these characteristics of God in your life?

DAY 2

2 Chronicles 7:14

God's People

If my people, who are called by my name, will humble themselves and pray and seek my face and turn from their wicked ways, then will I hear from heaven and will forgive their sin and will heal their land.

Reflection Question:
What does God urge His people to do, and what are His promises when we do these things?

DAY 3

James 1:5

God's Wisdom

If any of you lacks wisdom, he should ask God, who gives generously to all without finding fault, and it will be given to him.

Reflection Question:
God has invited us to ask for wisdom. Take a moment and ask for God's wisdom.

DAY 4

Philippians 4:6-7
God's Restoration

⁶ *Do not be anxious about anything, but in everything, by prayer and petition, with thanksgiving, present your requests to God.* ⁷ *And the peace of God, which transcends all understanding, will guard your hearts and your minds in Christ Jesus.*

Reflection Question:
God says He wants to hear your requests. How does this Scripture inspire you to talk to God honestly about yourself and your circumstances?

DAY 5

2 Timothy 3:16
God's Word

All Scripture is God-breathed and is useful for teaching, rebuking, correcting and training in righteousness.

Reflection Question:
What five things does this passage say about Scripture? Ask God to give you a deeper understanding of His character through His Word.

WEEKLY MEMORY VERSE

⁶ DO NOT BE ANXIOUS ABOUT ANYTHING, BUT IN EVERYTHING, BY PRAYER AND PETITION, WITH THANKSGIVING, PRESENT YOUR REQUESTS TO GOD. ⁷ AND THE PEACE OF GOD, WHICH TRANSCENDS ALL UNDERSTANDING, WILL GUARD YOUR HEARTS AND YOUR MINDS IN CHRIST JESUS.

PHILIPPIANS 4:6-7

WEEK 2

INTRODUCTION

The books of the prophets are often avoided. The history is unfamiliar. The names are hard to pronounce. The circumstances seem far removed from our lives. Somehow the messages seem too difficult to decipher. While it may be tempting to label the prophetic material as non-essential and relegate such studies to the scholars, it would be a significant oversight and limit our understanding of the Bible. Jesus was a Hebrew prophet. Moses was a prophet. It would be very difficult to understand the story of the Bible without understanding the roles of Jesus or Moses.

THE PROPHETS

The prophets are some of the most colorful characters of the story. Often the prophets were unpopular; the messages they brought were unwelcome. The prophetic literature reminds us of God's concern with His people and the events of their lives. God does not stand removed from history. God's people are at the center of His activity in the earth. The prophets enable us to understand God's perspective on the unfolding narrative of Scripture.

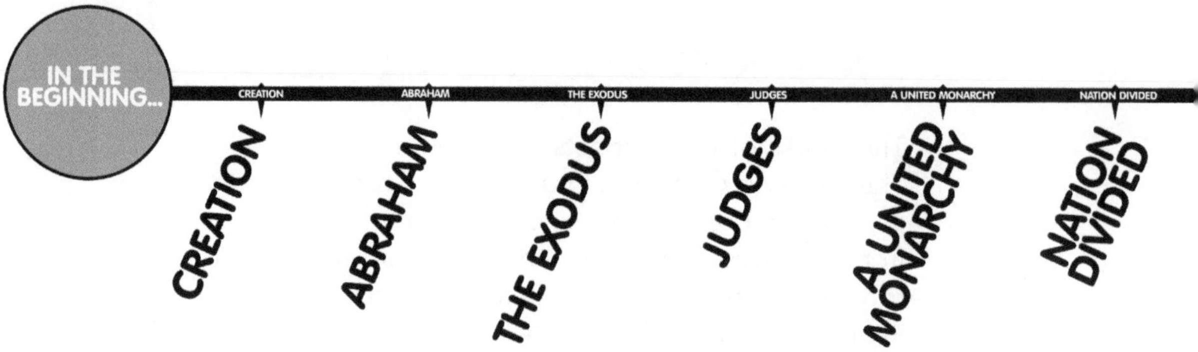

IN THE BEGINNING...

CREATION — ABRAHAM — THE EXODUS — JUDGES — A UNITED MONARCHY — NATION DIVIDED

CREATION

ABRAHAM

THE EXODUS

JUDGES

A UNITED MONARCHY

NATION DIVIDED

GETTING STARTED

Begin the session with a question below or brief activity to become better acquainted with one another.

1 What was the last book of the Bible you read?

2 Which translation do you prefer to read?

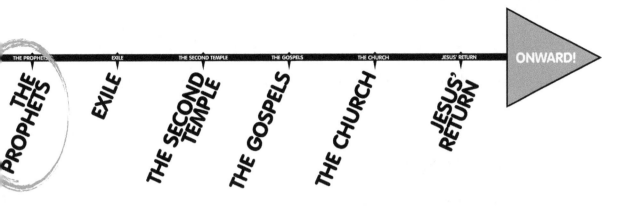

THE PROPHETS   EXILE   THE SECOND TEMPLE   THE GOSPELS   THE CHURCH   JESUS' RETURN   ONWARD!

OUTLINE OF DVD LESSON

Use the outline below to follow along during the DVD.

I. The Messengers

A. Prophet, Priest, and King
1. Prophet—represents God to people
2. Priest—represents humanity to God
3. King—authority and administration

B. Prophets in Scripture vs. Books of Prophecy
1. "Within the narrative"—Nathan, Elijah, Elisha, etc.
2. Major prophets—Isaiah, Jeremiah, Lamentations, Ezekiel, Daniel
3. Minor prophets—Hosea, Joel, Amos, Obadiah, Jonah, Micah, Nahum, Habakkuk, Zephaniah, Haggai, Zechariah, Malachi

C. Diverse Messages
1. Words of comfort
2. Words of challenge

D. False Prophets
Matthew 7:15-17

¹⁵ "Watch out for false prophets. They come to you in sheep's clothing, but inwardly they are ferocious wolves."

E. Two Greatest Prophets

II. Understanding/Believing Prophecy

Matthew 1:20-24

*²⁰ But after he had considered this, an angel of the Lord appeared to him in a dream and said, "Joseph son of David, do not be afraid to take Mary home as your wife, because what is conceived in her is from the Holy Spirit. ²¹ She will give birth to a son, and you are to give him the name Jesus, because he will save his people from their sins." ²² **All this took place to fulfill what the Lord had said through the prophet:** ²³ **"The virgin will be with child*** and will give birth to a son, and they will call him Immanuel"—which means, "God with us." ²⁴ When Joseph woke up, he did what the angel of the Lord had commanded him and took Mary home as his wife.

III. The Prophets

A. Unpleasant Assignments
Hosea 1:1-2 (NASB)

¹ The word of the LORD which came to Hosea the son of Beeri, during the days of Uzziah, Jotham, Ahaz and Hezekiah, kings of Judah, and during the days of Jeroboam the son of Joash, king of Israel. ² When the LORD first spoke through Hosea, the LORD said to Hosea, "Go, take to yourself a wife of harlotry and have children of harlotry; for the land commits flagrant harlotry, forsaking the LORD."

B. Sent to the Nations
Jonah 1:1-3

¹ The word of the LORD came to Jonah son of Amittai: ² "Go to the great city of Nineveh and preach against it, because its wickedness has come up before me." ³ But Jonah ran away from the LORD and headed for Tarshish. He went down to Joppa, where he found a ship bound for that port. After paying the fare, he went aboard and sailed for Tarshish to flee from the LORD.

Jonah 4:1-4

¹ But Jonah was greatly displeased and became angry. ² He prayed to the LORD, "O LORD, is this not what I said when I was still at home? That is why I was so quick to flee to Tarshish. I knew that you are a gracious and compassionate God, slow to anger and abounding in love, a God who relents from sending calamity. ³ Now, O LORD, take away my life, for it is better for me to die than to live." ⁴ But the LORD replied, "Have you any right to be angry?"

C. Bivocational
Amos 1:1-2

¹ The words of Amos, one of the shepherds of Tekoa—what he saw concerning Israel two years before the earthquake, when Uzziah was king of Judah and Jeroboam son of Jehoash was king of Israel. ² He said: "The LORD roars from Zion and thunders from Jerusalem; the pastures of the shepherds dry up, and the top of Carmel withers."

D. Very "Human"

1 Kings 19:13-18

[13] When Elijah heard it, he pulled his cloak over his face and went out and stood at the mouth of the cave. Then a voice said to him, "What are you doing here, Elijah?" [14] He replied, "I have been very zealous for the LORD God Almighty. The Israelites have rejected your covenant, broken down your altars, and put your prophets to death with the sword. I am the only one left, and now they are trying to kill me too." [15] The LORD said to him, "Go back the way you came, and go to the Desert of Damascus. When you get there, anoint Hazael king over Aram. [18] Yet I reserve seven thousand in Israel—all whose knees have not bowed down to Baal and all whose mouths have not kissed him."

Galatians 6:7-9

[7] Do not be deceived: God cannot be mocked. A man reaps what he sows. [8] The one who sows to please his sinful nature, from that nature will reap destruction; the one who sows to please the Spirit, from the Spirit will reap eternal life. [9] Let us not become weary in doing good, for at the proper time we will reap a harvest if we do not give up.

BUT WHEN IT WAS GOD'S TURN...

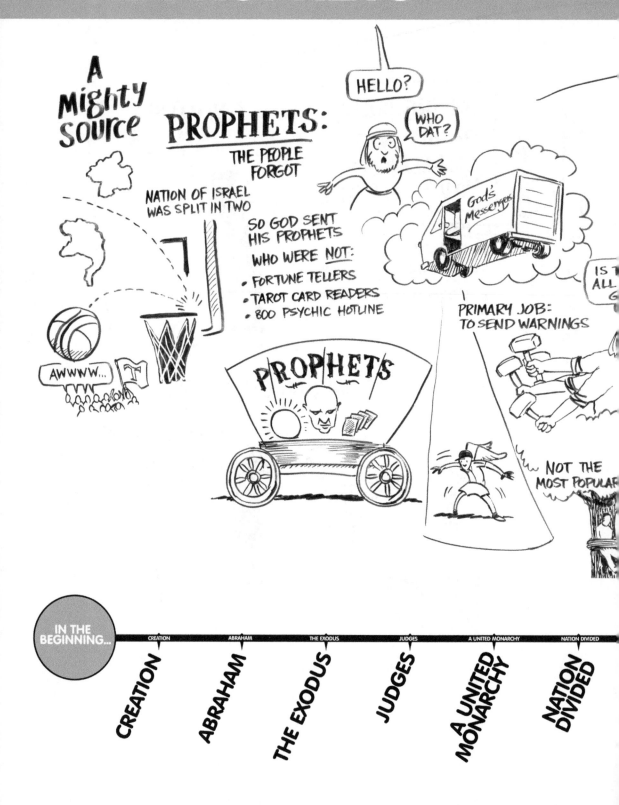

A Mighty Source

PROPHETS: THE PEOPLE FORGOT

HELLO?

WHO DAT?

NATION OF ISRAEL WAS SPLIT IN TWO

SO GOD SENT HIS PROPHETS WHO WERE NOT:
- FORTUNE TELLERS
- TAROT CARD READERS
- 800 PSYCHIC HOTLINE

God's Messenger

IS T ALL G

AWWWW...

PROPHETS

PRIMARY JOB: TO SEND WARNINGS

NOT THE MOST POPULAR

IN THE BEGINNING...

CREATION   ABRAHAM   THE EXODUS   JUDGES   A UNITED MONARCHY   NATION DIVIDED

CREATION

ABRAHAM

THE EXODUS

JUDGES

A UNITED MONARCHY

NATION DIVIDED

THE PROPHETS   EXILE   THE SECOND TEMPLE   THE GOSPELS   THE CHURCH   JESUS' RETURN   ONWARD!

THE PROPHETS   EXILE   THE SECOND TEMPLE   THE GOSPELS   THE CHURCH   JESUS' RETURN

DISCUSSION

Using the questions that follow, we will review and expand on the teaching we just experienced.

1 Define the role of the prophet.

2 What was the focus of the priests?

3 What is the primary assignment of the king?

4 Which of these roles is most prominent in contemporary life?

Hosea 1:1-2 (NASB)

1 The word of the Lord which came to Hosea the son of Beeri, during the days of Uzziah, Jotham, Ahaz and Hezekiah, kings of Judah, and during the days of Jeroboam the son of Joash, king of Israel. 2 When the Lord first spoke through Hosea, the Lord said to Hosea, "Go, take to yourself a wife of harlotry and have children of harlotry; for the land commits flagrant harlotry, forsaking the Lord."

5 Why did God give Hosea such an unusual assignment?

6 Hosea's God-assignment was a very direct confrontation to the behavior of Israel. What do you imagine God would say to the Church in our generation?

A MIGHTY SOURCE

PROPHETS:
THE PEOPLE FORGOT

NATION OF ISRAEL WAS SPLIT IN TWO

SO GOD SENT HIS PROPHETS WHO WERE NOT:
• FORTUNE TELLERS
• TAROT CARD READERS
• 800 PSYCHIC HOTLINE

AWWWW...

PROPHETS

APPLICATION

Now it's time to make some personal applications of all we've been thinking about in the last few minutes.

READ ALOUD

The prophets delivered a God-perspective to the people. Sometimes the messages were about divine deliverance. At other times the messages were about discipline or judgment. The tasks often required the prophets to stand against popular opinion. Just because God issues the assignment does not mean it is always fun or pleasant. The prophets faced the same challenges that God's people confront in every generation—weariness, fear, discouragement, and even persecution. One of the lessons of the prophets is that serving God is not always about comfort and convenience.

Elijah had a tremendous victory on Mt. Carmel. God sent fire from heaven to validate the message Elijah had delivered. Then Elijah prayed and God sent rain to end a three-year drought. Still, Elijah had to face the anger and threats of Jezebel. God's presence did not remove him from the conflict or the stress of confrontation.

1 Kings 18:36-39

³⁶ At the time of sacrifice, the prophet Elijah stepped forward and prayed: "O LORD, God of Abraham, Isaac and Israel, let it be known today that you are God in Israel and that I am your servant and have done all these things at your command. ³⁷ Answer me, O LORD, answer me, so these people will know that you, O LORD, are God, and that you are turning their hearts back again." ³⁸ Then the fire of the LORD fell and burned up the sacrifice, the wood, the stones and the soil, and also licked up the water in the trench. ³⁹ When all the people saw this, they fell prostrate and cried, "The LORD— he is God! The LORD—he is God!"

7 Elijah's boldness resulted in a change of heart for many Israelites. Describe a time when someone's boldness enabled you to choose God's way more readily.

1 Kings 18:44-46

44 The seventh time the servant reported, "A cloud as small as a man's hand is rising from the sea." So Elijah said, "Go and tell Ahab, 'Hitch up your chariot and go down before the rain stops you.'" 45 Meanwhile, the sky grew black with clouds, the wind rose, a heavy rain came on and Ahab rode off to Jezreel. 46 The power of the LORD came upon Elijah and, tucking his cloak into his belt, he ran ahead of Ahab all the way to Jezreel.

8 Elijah prayed and boldly declared it would rain after a lengthy drought. Prayers open doors of possibility for God. Take a few moments and share a time when God's response to prayer impacted your life.

41

1 Kings 19:1-3

1 Now Ahab told Jezebel everything Elijah had done and how he had killed all the prophets with the sword. 2 So Jezebel sent a messenger to Elijah to say, "May the gods deal with me, be it ever so severely, if by this time tomorrow I do not make your life like that of one of them." 3 Elijah was afraid and ran for his life.

9 God's power did not cause His enemies to withdraw. They were more aggressive. What did Jezebel promise? How did Elijah respond? Are these the outcomes you would have anticipated after God rained fire from heaven?

> **1 Kings 19:3-5**
>
> [3] Elijah was afraid and ran for his life. When he came to Beersheba in Judah, he left his servant there, [4] while he himself went a day's journey into the desert. He came to a broom tree, sat down under it and prayed that he might die. "I have had enough, LORD," he said. "Take my life; I am no better than my ancestors." [5] Then he lay down under the tree and fell asleep. All at once an angel touched him and said, "Get up and eat."

10 Elijah fled to the desert. How would you describe Elijah's mood?

> **1 Kings 19:5-8**
>
> [5] Then he lay down under the tree and fell asleep. All at once an angel touched him and said, "Get up and eat." [6] He looked around, and there by his head was a cake of bread baked over hot coals, and a jar of water. He ate and drank and then lay down again. [7] The angel of the LORD came back a second time and touched him and said, "Get up and eat, for the journey is too much for you." [8] So he got up and ate and drank. Strengthened by that food, he traveled forty days and forty nights until he reached Horeb, the mountain of God.

11 The physical, emotional, and spiritual demands of confronting evil left Elijah exhausted. How did God respond to him?

READ ALOUD

The biblical picture of serving God extends far beyond attending worship services. The prophets primarily addressed God's people, not pagan nations, because there was consistent need for God's people to be redirected toward their faith. It seems the temptations to selfishness and ungodliness are consistent through history. God needs a voice in every generation to remind His people of His purposes for them.

12 With Elijah as an example, what can we anticipate when we are advocates for Jesus in our generation?

13 When you have been convicted about ungodliness in your own life, how did you feel about the messenger?

14 Discuss ways you can allow your faith to be more prominent. Before you dismiss, ask God to give you a spirit of boldness and courage.

PRAYER

Close the session in prayer. Share prayer requests with the group, and pray for each other. Close by praying the following prayer together.

Heavenly Father, thank You for watching over our lives and being concerned for our well-being. Forgive us for being lukewarm and distracted. Awaken us to Your purposes. Open our eyes to see the world around us from Your perspective. Help us to see the people in our lives with Your compassion. As we open our hearts to Your Word, let Your power be made evident in our lives. Through our efforts may the name of Jesus be lifted up and His Kingdom extended. In Jesus' name, amen.

Prayer requests this week:

GOING DEEPER

This section is designed to do as homework, if you choose, between your Small Group meetings.

....

Isaiah's Commissioning

Isaiah 6:1-8

¹ In the year that King Uzziah died, I saw the Lord seated on a throne, high and exalted, and the train of his robe filled the temple. ² Above him were seraphs, each with six wings: With two wings they covered their faces, with two they covered their feet, and with two they were flying. ³ And they were calling to one another: "Holy, holy, holy is the LORD Almighty; the whole earth is full of his glory." ⁴ At the sound of their voices the doorposts and thresholds shook and the temple was filled with smoke.

⁵ "Woe to me!" I cried. "I am ruined! For I am a man of unclean lips, and I live among a people of unclean lips, and my eyes have seen the King, the LORD Almighty." ⁶ Then one of the seraphs flew to me with a live coal in his hand, which he had taken with tongs from the altar. ⁷ With it he touched my mouth and said, "See, this has touched your lips; your guilt is taken away and your sin atoned for." ⁸ Then I heard the voice of the Lord saying, "Whom shall I send? And who will go for us?" And I said, "Here am I. Send me!"

Isaiah was a prophet in Jerusalem. He served under four kings of Judah: Uzziah, Jotham, Ahaz, and Hezekiah (Isaiah 1:1). The beauty and majesty of Isaiah's language make his writings a favorite of many. Isaiah 53 is a powerful presentation of the Messiah who redeems all. In this first chapter, we are invited into the throne room of God and are privileged to listen and observe as Isaiah receives his commission.

- Read verses 1-4. Isaiah enters into the throne room of God. What are the sights and sounds he experiences?

- In the Hebrew language, repetition is a way of adding emphasis. What attribute of God is emphasized in this majestic presentation?

- When confronted with the holiness of God, what is Isaiah's first insight?

- Read Luke 5:4-8. What was Peter's reaction when he was confronted with the majesty and power of Jesus?

- In verse 7 the angel places a hot coal on Isaiah's lips. Read James 3:2-8. James tells us that we should strive to keep our tongue under control in order to do what?

- God cleansed and prepared Isaiah for his assignment. Read 1 John 1:9. How can we cooperate with God to be prepared?

- Isaiah volunteered to serve the Lord. Reflect on your willingness to serve the Lord and His people.

DAILY REFLECTIONS

These are daily reviews of the key Bible verses and related others that will help you think about and apply the insights from this session.

DAY 1

Ezekiel 36:25-27

God's Benefits

25 I will sprinkle clean water on you, and you will be clean; I will cleanse you from all your impurities and from all your idols. 26 I will give you a new heart and put a new spirit in you; I will remove from you your heart of stone and give you a heart of flesh. 27 And I will put my Spirit in you and move you to follow my decrees and be careful to keep my laws."

Reflection Question:
List the great benefits God has for you. Whom do you need to welcome into your life in order to obtain God's benefits?

DAY 2

1 Corinthians 2:9-10

Who Knew?

9 However, as it is written: "No eye has seen, no ear has heard, no mind has conceived what God has prepared for those who love him"—10 but God has revealed it to us by his Spirit. The Spirit searches all things, even the deep things of God.

Reflection Question:
Where do you need a God-sized outcome? Would you recognize the Holy Spirit's work in your life? Have you embraced the Holy Spirit and invited Him to be your teacher?

DAY 3

Psalm 33:11

Confidence

But the plans of the LORD stand firm forever, the purposes of his heart through all generations.

Reflective Question:
Applying this verse in a practical way demands that you know something about God's past job performance. What can you do to understand your Bible more completely?

DAY 4

Hosea 6:6

Repentance

"For I desire mercy, not sacrifice, and acknowledgment of God rather than burnt offerings."

Reflection Question:
What is the difference between outward observances and sincere repentance?

_____

_____

_____

_____

_____

_____

DAY 5

John 14:23

Obedience

Jesus replied, "If anyone loves me, he will obey my teaching. My Father will love him, and we will come to him and make our home with him."

Reflection Question:
How does God know if you love Him? How important is it for you to have the Father's love in your life?

_____

_____

_____

_____

_____

WEEKLY MEMORY VERSE

BUT THE PLANS OF THE LORD STAND FIRM FOREVER, THE PURPOSES OF HIS HEART THROUGH ALL GENERATIONS.

PSALM 33:11

WEEK 3

INTRODUCTION

The Bible reveals to us the process of God's preparing a people. In Genesis 12, God promised Abraham he would bring forth a nation. In the unfolding story we are invited to witness the incredible drama of the emergence of the Hebrew people: their delivery from slavery under Egyptian oppression, an impossible story of provision through a wilderness journey, the conquest of the Promised Land, and eventually the establishment of the Israelite monarchy. God's promises, however, are not without condition. The

THE EXILE

Israelites' privilege of dwelling in the Promised Land was linked to their obedience. Persistent rebellion and the refusal to accept God's discipline or heed the warnings of the prophets resulted in being expelled from their land. Even in this time of discipline, God's grace was evident in the lives of His people. From the ghettos of Babylon, the Jewish people returned to rebuild Jerusalem and build a second temple. The story of God's watching over His people continues.

IN THE BEGINNING...

CREATION ABRAHAM THE EXODUS JUDGES A UNITED MONARCHY NATION DIVIDED

CREATION

ABRAHAM

THE EXODUS

JUDGES

A UNITED MONARCHY

NATION DIVIDED

52 GETTING STARTED

Begin the session with a question below or brief activity to become better acquainted with one another.

1 Share the most significant thing you have learned from the study so far.

2 Describe a time when you were chosen.

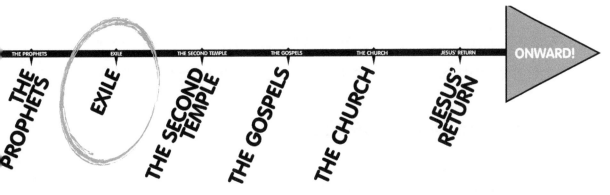

OUTLINE OF DVD LESSON

Use the outline below to follow along during the DVD.

I. A Nation Divided (922 B C)

A. Israel, the Northern Kingdom
B. Judah, the Southern Kingdom

II. Tragedy

A. Israel Conquered by Assyrians, 721 B C
B. Judah Conquered by Babylonians, 587 B C

III. The Exile

Psalm 137:1-6

¹ By the rivers of Babylon we sat and wept when we remembered Zion. ² There on the poplars we hung our harps, ³ for there our captors asked us for songs, our tormentors demanded songs of joy; they said, "Sing us one of the songs of Zion!" ⁴ How can we sing the songs of the LORD while in a foreign land? ⁵ If I forget you, O Jerusalem, may my right hand forget its skill. ⁶ May my tongue cling to the roof of my mouth if I do not remember you, if I do not consider Jerusalem my highest joy.

A. God's Promise
Jeremiah 31:10-13

¹⁰ "Hear the word of the LORD, O nations; proclaim it in distant coastlands: 'He who scattered Israel will gather them and will watch over his flock like a shepherd.' ¹¹ For the LORD will ransom Jacob and redeem them from the hand of those stronger than they. ¹² They will come and shout for joy on the heights of Zion; they will rejoice in the bounty of the Lord—the grain, the new wine and the oil, the young of the flocks and herds. They will be like a well-watered garden, and they will sorrow no more. ¹³ Then maidens will dance and be glad, young men and old as well. I will turn their mourning into gladness; I will give them comfort and joy instead of sorrow.

B. God's Presence, Power, and Provision

1. Daniel

Daniel 1:17

To these four young men God gave knowledge and understanding of all kinds of literature and learning. And Daniel could understand visions and dreams of all kinds.

2. Esther

Esther 2:17-18

[17] Now the king was attracted to Esther more than to any of the other women, and she won his favor and approval more than any of the other virgins. So he set a royal crown on her head and made her queen instead of Vashti. [18] And the king gave a great banquet, Esther's banquet, for all his nobles and officials. He proclaimed a holiday throughout the provinces and distributed gifts with royal liberality.

Esther 4:12-16

[12] When Esther's words were reported to Mordecai, [13] he sent back this answer: "Do not think that because you are in the king's house you alone of all the Jews will escape. [14] For if you remain silent at this time, relief and deliverance for the Jews will arise from another place, but you and your father's family will perish. And who knows but that you have come to royal position for such a time as this?" [15] Then Esther sent this reply to Mordecai: [16] "Go, gather together all the Jews who are in Susa, and fast for me. Do not eat or drink for three days, night or day. I and my maids will fast as you do. When this is done, I will go to the king, even though it is against the law. And if I perish, I perish."

THE EXILE

A MIGHTY *Source*

EXILE

THE BIBLE HAS ITS SHARE OF TRAGEDY

GOD WARNED THE ISRAELITES TIME AND TIME AGAIN, BUT THEY WOULDN'T LISTEN

JUST A HEADS-UP...

NANANANANA... I CAN'T **HEAR** YOUUUU...

SO GOD ALLOWED ASSYRIA TO CONQUER ISRAEL IN THE NORTH

BUT A REMNANT STILL TRUSTED GOD AND REMEMBERED THE PROPHETS

WE SHOULD HAVE LISTENED!

AND BABYLON TO CONQUER JUDAH IN THE SOUTH

WE SHOULD HAVE LISTENED

AND COMM TO FOLLO

BUCKET O'SAD

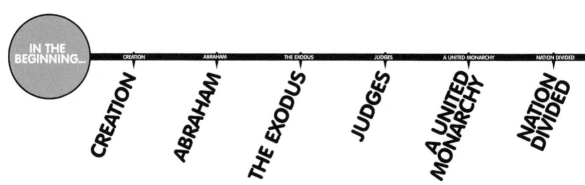

IN THE BEGINNING...

CREATION — ABRAHAM — THE EXODUS — JUDGES — A UNITED MONARCHY — NATION DIVIDED

CREATION

ABRAHAM

THE EXODUS

JUDGES

A UNITED MONARCHY

NATION DIVIDED

DISCUSSION

Using the questions that follow, we will review and expand on the teaching we just experienced.

READ ALOUD

The Exile refers to the period in Israelite history when they were overcome by enemy nations and driven out of the Land of Promise. Being chosen by God does not remove us from the responsibility of obedience and faithfulness. God's discipline is an expression of His love. Through the tragedy of defeat and exile emerged a remarkable new future for Israel and the Jewish people.

1 Israel was defeated in 721 BC by which nation?

2 Judah was conquered in 587 BC by which Babylonian king?

3 Who constructed the first temple in Jerusalem?

THE **WHITEBOARD** BIBLE

4   Babylonian destruction of the temple was a startling event. The symbol of God's abiding presence was removed. How was God's power demonstrated to His people while in Babylon?

Jeremiah 25:8-11

8 Therefore the LORD Almighty says this: "Because you have not listened to my words, 9 I will summon all the peoples of the north and my servant Nebuchadnezzar king of Babylon," declares the LORD,...
11 "This whole country will become a desolate wasteland, and these nations will serve the king of Babylon seventy years."

5   The Israelites were defeated, not by the strength of an adversary, but because they refused to cooperate with their protector. What did God identify as the primary problem?

Psalm 137:1-9

1 By the rivers of Babylon we sat and wept when we remembered Zion. 2 There on the poplars we hung our harps, 3 for there our captors asked us for songs, our tormentors demanded songs of joy; they said, "Sing us one of the songs of Zion!" 4 How can we sing the songs of the LORD while in a foreign land? 5 If I forget you, O Jerusalem, may my right hand forget its skill. 6 May my tongue cling to the roof of my mouth if I do not remember you, if I do not consider Jerusalem my highest joy. 7 Remember, O LORD, what the Edomites did on the day Jerusalem fell. "Tear it down," they cried, "tear it down to its foundations!" 8 O Daughter of Babylon, doomed to destruction, happy is he who repays you for what you have done to us—9 he who seizes your infants and dashes them against the rocks.

6   Jerusalem is at the heart of Israel's understanding of God's promise. Their restoration of favor with God is inseparable from the city of Jerusalem. God's promise is eternal. How is this promise a part of contemporary world events? What lessons can we learn from this Scripture?

APPLICATION

Now it's time to make some personal applications of all we've been thinking about in the last few minutes.

READ ALOUD

The Exile was a time of great despair and difficulty. It was also a very fruitful time in Israelite history. The fear of being assimilated resulted in a focused effort to keep their story and honor the covenants with God. The remembrance of the Exodus and God's provision in the wilderness presented hope that God would once again restore His people.

Jeremiah 31:10-13

10 "Hear the word of the LORD, O nations; proclaim it in distant coastlands: 'He who scattered Israel will gather them and will watch over his flock like a shepherd.' 11 For the LORD will ransom Jacob and redeem them from the hand of those stronger than they. 12 They will come and shout for joy on the heights of Zion; they will rejoice in the bounty of the LORD—the grain, the new wine and the oil, the young of the flocks and herds. They will be like a well-watered garden, and they will sorrow no more. 13 Then maidens will dance and be glad, young men and old as well. I will turn their mourning into gladness; I will give them comfort and joy instead of sorrow.

7 Jeremiah was the prophet who unrelentingly warned of Babylon's coming and Jerusalem's destruction. Yet, from the shadow of impending destruction, Jeremiah held out hope of God's restoration. How would hope of a future enable perseverance?

Daniel 9:1-2

[1] In the first year of Darius son of Xerxes (a Mede by descent), who was made ruler over the Babylonian kingdom—[2] in the first year of his reign, I, Daniel, understood from the Scriptures, according to the word of the LORD given to Jeremiah the prophet, that the desolation of Jerusalem would last seventy years.

8 Daniel studied Jeremiah and realized the exile would last only seventy years. What can we anticipate in our future from the study of Scripture? What would Daniel have forfeited if he had not read or believed Jeremiah? What do we forfeit by ignoring God's Word?

READ ALOUD

God's power was manifest in the lives of His people even during captivity. It is a powerful reminder that when circumstances are difficult or life is painful, God's power is present to help us. Great victories emerge from great threats.

Daniel 6:21-22, 26-28

[21] Daniel answered, "O king, live forever! [22] My God sent his angel, and he shut the mouths of the lions. They have not hurt me, because I was found innocent in his sight. Nor have I ever done any wrong before you, O king." [26] "I issue a decree that in every part of my kingdom people must fear and reverence the God of Daniel. "For he is the living God and he endures forever; his kingdom will not be destroyed, his dominion will never end. [27] He rescues and he saves; he performs signs and wonders in the heavens and on the earth. He has rescued Daniel from the power of the lions." [28] So Daniel prospered during the reign of Darius and the reign of Cyrus the Persian.

9 Tragedy and triumph both accurately describe Daniel's life. Honoring God when circumstances are difficult is part of our assignment. Discuss the struggle to honor God, even when He is not alleviating all suffering.

10 Daniel honored God even when threatened. What was the result of Daniel's faithfulness?

THE **WHITEBOARD** BIBLE

READ ALOUD

Esther became Queen of Persia. However, she had hidden her ethnicity. She faced a dilemma; to help her people she would risk her own safety. Her remarkable courage changed the course of an empire.

Esther 4:12-16

12 When Esther's words were reported to Mordecai, 13 he sent back this answer: "Do not think that because you are in the king's house you alone of all the Jews will escape. 14 For if you remain silent at this time, relief and deliverance for the Jews will arise from another place, but you and your father's family will perish. And who knows but that you have come to royal position for such a time as this?" 15 Then Esther sent this reply to Mordecai: 16 "Go, gather together all the Jews who are in Susa, and fast for me. Do not eat or drink for three days, night or day. I and my maids will fast as you do. When this is done, I will go to the king, even though it is against the law. And if I perish, I perish."

11 What was Mordecai's reminder to Esther?

12 What privileges has God invested in your life? What responsibilities toward God and His people are implied?

READ ALOUD

It is easy to look at the failure of the Church and be critical. It takes faith to look at our world and believe God is restoring His people. We have the privilege of trusting God and seeing His purposes emerge in our generation.

13 How does understanding the story of the Bible help you to be faithful in the midst of your life's circumstances?

BUT GOD
PROTECTED
THEM

PRAYER

Close the session in prayer. Share prayer requests with the group, and pray for each other. Close by praying the following prayer together.

Heavenly Father, we pray today for the peace of Jerusalem. We come as "watchmen on the walls" to cry out on behalf of Israel and Your people throughout the earth. Be merciful to those who are enduring. May those who oppose Your purposes be confused and ineffective. Raise up men and women of strength and courage to lead Your people. Send Your angels to intervene on our behalf. Allow our lives to bring glory and honor to our Lord Jesus. In Jesus name, amen.

Prayer requests this week:

GOING DEEPER

This section is designed to do as homework, if you choose, between your Small Group meetings.

. . . .

Learn from Daniel's Obedience

Daniel 1:3-17

3 Then the king ordered Ashpenaz, chief of his court officials, to bring in some of the Israelites from the royal family and the nobility—4 young men without any physical defect, handsome, showing aptitude for every kind of learning, well informed, quick to understand, and qualified to serve in the king's palace. He was to teach them the language and literature of the Babylonians. 5 The king assigned them a daily amount of food and wine from the king's table. They were to be trained for three years, and after that they were to enter the king's service. 6 Among these were some from Judah: Daniel, Hananiah, Mishael and Azariah. 7 The chief official gave them new names: to Daniel, the name Belteshazzar; to Hananiah, Shadrach; to Mishael, Meshach; and to Azariah, Abednego. 8 But Daniel resolved not to defile himself with the royal food and wine, and he asked the chief official for permission not to defile himself this way. 9 Now God had caused the official to show favor and sympathy to Daniel, 10 but the official told Daniel, "I am afraid of my lord the king, who has assigned your food and drink. Why should he see you looking worse than the other young men your age? The king would then have my head because of you." 11 Daniel then said to the guard whom the chief official had appointed over Daniel, Hananiah, Mishael and Azariah, 12 "Please test your servants for ten days: Give us nothing but vegetables to eat and water to drink. 13 Then compare our appearance with that of the young men who eat the royal food, and treat your servants in accordance with what you see." 14 So he agreed to this and tested them for ten days. 15 At the end of the ten days they looked healthier and better nourished than any of the young men who ate the royal food. 16 So the guard took away their choice food and the wine they were to drink and gave them vegetables instead. 17 To these four young men God gave knowledge and understanding of all kinds of literature and learning. And Daniel could understand visions and dreams of all kinds.

READ ALOUD

Daniel and his friends had been taken from Jerusalem to Babylon. They had experienced defeat, destruction, and the dismantling of their life dreams. Then they were selected to serve the royal court. Their responses provide insight and challenges for us.

- Every part of their life and faith was being challenged. List some of the changes they were facing.

- Daniel chose to maintain his "kosher diet," an amazing expression of obedience in the face of bitter disappointment. How does disappointment affect your responses to God?

- Read Galatians 6:9. What causes us to give up? What is our motivation for not giving up?

- Learning to persevere is an indication of maturity—physically, emotionally, and spiritually. Read James 1:2-4. What are the requirements for maturity and completion?

- What did God do for these four young men in response to their faithfulness?

- Read James 1:5. What does God give us permission to ask for?

- Availability and obedience are more important than ability. Reflect on the places you are struggling with disappointments and obedience. Ask the Holy Spirit to give you wisdom to persevere so that you do not forfeit the good things God has for you.

DAILY REFLECTIONS

These are daily reviews of the key Bible verses and related others that will help you think about and apply the insights from this session.

DAY 1

Jeremiah 31:10b

God's Promise

"'He who scattered Israel will gather them and will watch over his flock like a shepherd.'"

Reflection Question:
Consider the keeping power of God and His watchfulness over our lives. In what ways do we minimize these characteristics of God?

DAY 2

Daniel 6:26-27

Ambassadors

"For he is the living God and he endures forever; his kingdom will not be destroyed, his dominion will never end. ²⁷ He rescues and he saves; he performs signs and wonders in the heavens and on the earth. He has rescued Daniel from the power of the lions."

Reflection Question:
King Darius made this statement because of Daniel's faithfulness. What do others say about God because of your faithfulness?

DAY 3

Esther 4:14

Privilege & Purpose

¹⁴ "For if you remain silent at this time, relief and deliverance for the Jews will arise from another place, but you and your father's family will perish. And who knows but that you have come to royal position for such a time as this?"

Reflection Question:
In what ways have you used your position or gifts for the service of God?

DAY 4

Psalm 137:5-6
Never Forget

⁵ If I forget you, O Jerusalem, may my right hand forget its skill.
⁶ May my tongue cling to the roof of my mouth if I do not remember you, if I do not consider Jerusalem my highest joy.

Reflection Question:
After being exiled from their land, the Jewish people made the above statement of faith in order to never forget the purposes and plans of God. What are you doing to remember God's plan for your life?

_____

_____

_____

DAY 5

Psalm 122:6
God Cares for Jerusalem

Pray for the peace of Jerusalem: "May those who love you be secure."

Reflection Question:
What does God instruct us to do in this passage? Take a moment to pray for the peace of Jerusalem.

_____

_____

_____

_____

_____

_____

WEEKLY MEMORY VERSE

PRAY FOR THE PEACE OF JERUSALEM: "MAY THOSE WHO LOVE YOU BE SECURE."

PSALM 122:6

WEEK 4

INTRODUCTION

The Wisdom Literature—The Writings—include the books of Job, Psalms, Proverbs, Ecclesiastes, and the Song of Solomon. These books are typically more familiar to us. They provide us with significant insight into the character of God and how He interacts with His people. These books offer God's wisdom for facing the challenges of life, reminders of God's faithfulness, and the certainty that God is watching over all things.

THE WISDOM LITERATURE 71

This session does not fit neatly into our timeline. The Wisdom Literature is a collection of writings and not just the work of one person or the record of a single event. Job is thought to be one of the oldest books of the Bible; some date the work as early as the time of Abraham. King David is credited with many of the Psalms. King Solomon collected proverbs and shared his wisdom in Ecclesiastes and the Song of Solomon. If a timeline point is helpful, the United Monarchy would be a good choice.

INTERESTING

YOU CAN LEARN MORE ABOUT THE STORY

THE WISDOM LITERATURE EXTENDS

IN THE BEGINNING...

CREATION   ABRAHAM   THE EXODUS   JUDGES   A UNITED MONARCHY   NATION DIVIDED

CREATION

ABRAHAM

THE EXODUS

JUDGES

A UNITED MONARCHY

NATION DIVIDED

GETTING STARTED

Begin the session with a question below or brief activity to become better acquainted with one another.

1 As a group, list the first ten books of the Bible.

2 Who is the wisest person you have known?

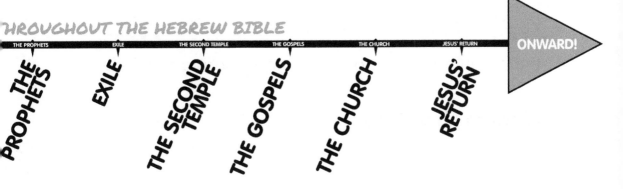

THROUGHOUT THE HEBREW BIBLE

THE PROPHETS   EXILE   THE SECOND TEMPLE   THE GOSPELS   THE CHURCH   JESUS' RETURN   ONWARD!

THE PROPHETS

EXILE

THE SECOND TEMPLE

THE GOSPELS

THE CHURCH

JESUS' RETURN

OUTLINE OF DVD LESSON

Use the outline below to follow along during the DVD.

I. Wisdom Literature

A. Job

Job 1:6-8

6 One day the angels came to present themselves before the LORD, and Satan also came with them. 7 The LORD said to Satan, "Where have you come from?" Satan answered the LORD, "From roaming through the earth and going back and forth in it." 8 Then the LORD said to Satan, "Have you considered my servant Job? There is no one on earth like him; he is blameless and upright, a man who fears God and shuns evil."

B. Psalms

Psalm 51:1-14

1 Have mercy on me, O God, according to your unfailing love; according to your great compassion blot out my transgressions. 2 Wash away all my iniquity and cleanse me from my sin. 3 For I know my transgressions, and my sin is always before me. 4 Against you, you only, have I sinned and done what is evil in your sight, so that you are proved right when you speak and justified when you judge. 5 Surely I was sinful at birth, sinful from the time my mother conceived me. 6 Surely you desire truth in the inner parts; you teach me wisdom in the inmost place. 7 Cleanse me with hyssop, and I will be clean; wash me, and I will be whiter than snow. 8 Let me hear joy and gladness; let the bones you have crushed rejoice. 9 Hide your face from my sins and blot out all my iniquity. 10 Create in me a pure heart, O God, and renew a steadfast spirit within me. 11 Do not cast me from your presence or take your Holy Spirit from me. 12 Restore to me the joy of your salvation and grant me a willing spirit, to sustain me. 13 Then I will teach transgressors your ways, and sinners will turn back to you. 14 Save me from bloodguilt, O God, the God who saves me, and my tongue will sing of your righteousness.

C. Proverbs

Proverbs 3:7-8

7 Do not be wise in your own eyes; fear the LORD and shun evil. 8 This will bring health to your body and nourishment to your bones.

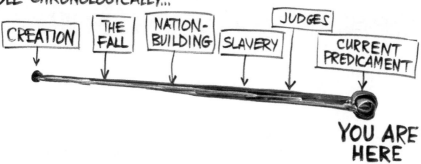

WE'VE BEEN LOOKING
AT THE STORY IN THE
BIBLE CHRONOLOGICALLY...

CREATION | THE FALL | NATION-BUILDING | SLAVERY | JUDGES | CURRENT PREDICAMENT

YOU ARE HERE

D. Ecclesiastes

Ecclesiastes 1:1-3

1 The words of the Teacher, son of David, king in Jerusalem: 2 "Meaningless! Meaningless!" says the Teacher. "Utterly meaningless! Everything is meaningless." 3 What does man gain from all his labor at which he toils under the sun?

THE WISDOM LITERATURE

A Mighty Source:

Wisdom Literature:

SOMETIMES IT HELPS TO LOOK AT THE STORY BEHIND THE STORY...

INTERESTING

YOU CAN LEARN MORE ABOUT THE STORY

SOME STORIES ARE SIMPLE:
- LITTLE RED RIDING HOOD
- THE UGLY DUCKLING

WE'VE BEEN LOOKING AT THE STORY IN THE BIBLE CHRONOLOGICALLY...

CREATION | THE FALL | NATION-BUILDING | SLAVERY | JUDGES | CURRENT PREDICAMENT

YOU ARE HERE

SOME STORIES ARE DIFFICULT:
- INCEPTION

WHAT'S THE KICK ON THIS LEVEL?

- ERASERHEAD (GRADUATE) LEVEL
- PASTOR ALLEN'S SERMONS

BUT OR TYP

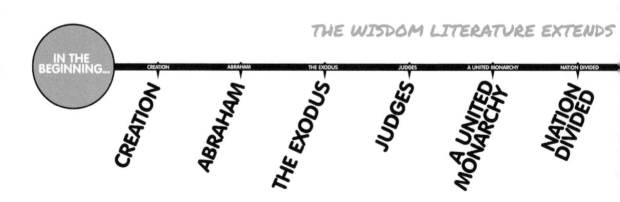

THE WISDOM LITERATURE EXTENDS

IN THE BEGINNING...

CREATION | ABRAHAM | THE EXODUS | JUDGES | A UNITED MONARCHY | NATION DIVIDED

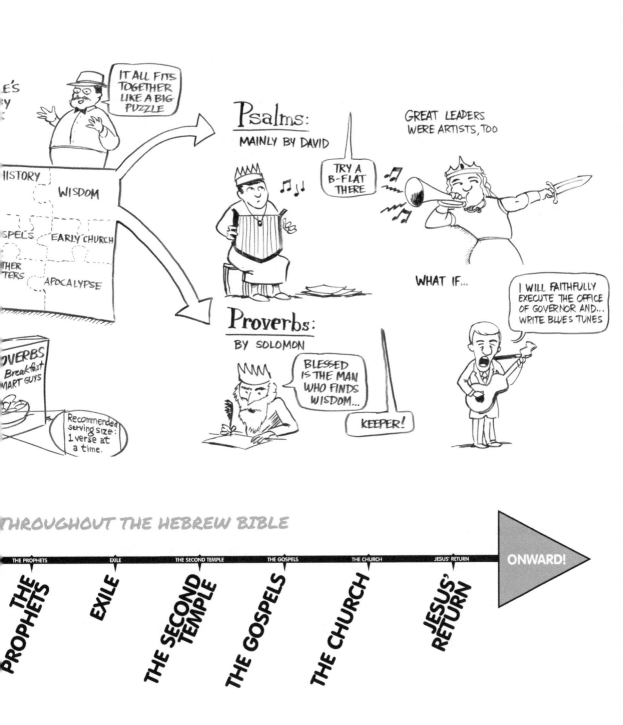

THROUGHOUT THE HEBREW BIBLE

THE PROPHETS · EXILE · THE SECOND TEMPLE · THE GOSPELS · THE CHURCH · JESUS' RETURN

THE PROPHETS · EXILE · THE SECOND TEMPLE · THE GOSPELS · THE CHURCH · JESUS' RETURN · ONWARD!

DISCUSSION

Using the questions that follow, we will review and expand on the teaching we just experienced.

....

READ ALOUD

Let's take a few moments and review the timeline. We have moved through much of the Old Testament. The ability to know a few key points provides a chronological framework enabling us to place characters and events into the biblical narrative. Learning a simple timeline can help a great deal in taking the mystery out of the Bible, providing a framework from which we can construct the story of God's preparing a people for Himself.

Ask a few volunteers to read each point on our timeline. Discuss highlights.

Creation—The beginning point of the entire story. It is not a fully formed account of original creation. The reader is invited into the story of God's dealing with the earth and specifically with Adam and his descendants.

Abraham—Genesis 12 is a significant turn in the unfolding story of the Bible. God begins to prepare a unique people. He makes a promise to Abraham that all people will be blessed through him.

Exodus—Genesis concludes with the extended family of Abraham arriving in Egypt. The second book of the Bible describes the deliverance from Egypt several hundred years later.

Judges—God raises up leaders to provide guidance for the tribes of Israel. God accepts responsibility for the well-being of His people.

The Monarchy—The Israelites want to be "like other nations" with a king to rule over them. God instructs Samuel, the last of the judges, to listen to them and anoint Saul as the first king of Israel.

A Nation Divided—After the death of Solomon, the nation of Israel is divided into two distinct nations. The northern kingdom is called Israel, with the capital city of Samaria. The southern kingdom is called Judah, with the capital of Jerusalem.

Prophets—Individuals chosen by God to deliver a message. At the heart of biblical prophecy is the presentation of a "God-perspective" to a chosen audience. The primary objective of prophecy is not predicting the future, although God does use the prophetic material to provide insight into His plans and purposes.

The Exile—Israel's right to dwell in the Promised Land is linked to their obedience to God. Persistent rebellion over many generations results in judgment, and God's people are defeated by their enemies. Israel was defeated by the Assyrians in 721 BC. Judah was defeated by the Babylonians in 587 BC.

1 Where in the Bible would you look for the story of Noah?

2 Who came first historically, King Saul or Moses?

3 In which book/books would you look for the story of David?

4 Who destroyed Solomon's temple in Jerusalem?

5 Which prophet consistently delivered the message of the Babylonian invasion?

APPLICATION

Now it's time to make some personal applications of all we've been thinking about in the last few minutes.

READ ALOUD

The book of Job explores the challenge of the suffering of the righteous. Job is a man celebrated by God, yet he endures much.

Job 1:6-12

⁶ One day the angels came to present themselves before the LORD, and Satan also came with them. ⁷ The LORD said to Satan, "Where have you come from?" Satan answered the LORD, "From roaming through the earth and going back and forth in it." ⁸ Then the LORD said to Satan, "Have you considered my servant Job? There is no one on earth like him; he is blameless and upright, a man who fears God and shuns evil." ⁹ "Does Job fear God for nothing?" Satan replied. ¹⁰ "Have you not put a hedge around him and his household and everything he has? You have blessed the work of his hands, so that his flocks and herds are spread throughout the land. ¹¹ But stretch out your hand and strike everything he has, and he will surely curse you to your face." ¹² The LORD said to Satan, "Very well, then, everything he has is in your hands, but on the man himself do not lay a finger." Then Satan went out from the presence of the LORD.

6 What does God say about Job?

7 What does Satan intend for Job?

READ ALOUD

The goodness of God and the destructive nature of Satan are clearly established. Yet we struggle to maintain this perspective, often imagining that God's plans will limit us and Satan's invitations will bring freedom and liberty.

Job 42:10, 12 (NASB)

¹⁰ The LORD restored the fortunes of Job when he prayed for his friends, and the LORD increased all that Job had twofold. ¹² The LORD blessed the latter days of Job more than his beginning.

8 Job experienced the faithfulness of God. Describe a time when you experienced the faithfulness of God's restoration.

READ ALOUD

The book of Psalms is the worship manual for the people of Israel. We are invited into the midst of God's dealings with His people. The literature is addressive; it speaks into our lives and brings hope, insight, and faith.

9 Do you have a favorite psalm? Tell which one and why.

Psalm 1:1-6

¹ Blessed is the man who does not walk in the counsel of the wicked or stand in the way of sinners or sit in the seat of mockers. ² But his delight is in the law of the LORD, and on his law he meditates day and night. ³ He is like a tree planted by streams of water, which yields its fruit in season and whose leaf does not wither. Whatever he does prospers. ⁴ Not so the wicked! They are like chaff that the wind blows away. ⁵ Therefore the wicked will not stand in the judgment, nor sinners in the assembly of the righteous. ⁶ For the LORD watches over the way of the righteous, but the way of the wicked will perish.

10 What does God promise the person who "delights in the law of the Lord"?

11 What is the outcome of the wicked?

READ ALOUD:

The book of Proverbs provides insight for living. We are given outcomes of life choices, enabling us to make wise choices.

Proverbs 3:7-8

7 Do not be wise in your own eyes; fear the LORD and shun evil. 8 This will bring health to your body and nourishment to your bones.

12 What will the fear of the Lord and shunning evil deliver to you?

Proverbs 22:4

Humility and the fear of the LORD bring wealth and honor and life.

13 How are we counseled to gain wealth, honor, and life?

READ ALOUD

If we have the humility to accept God's counsel, Proverbs will make the simple person wise.

PRAYER

Close the session in prayer. Share prayer requests with the group, and pray for each other. Close by praying the following prayer together.

Heavenly Father, thank You for the provision of Your Word. Grant me an understanding heart and a willing spirit. Holy Spirit, I choose to cooperate with Your instruction. Forgive me for resisting Your invitations. Teach me to put my trust fully in the God of Abraham, Isaac, and Jacob. In Jesus' name, amen.

Prayer requests this week:

GOING DEEPER

This section is designed to do as homework, if you choose, between your Small Group meetings.

Perseverance and Overcoming

Galatians 6:8-10

8 The one who sows to please his sinful nature, from that nature will reap destruction; the one who sows to please the Spirit, from the Spirit will reap eternal life. 9 Let us not become weary in doing good, for at the proper time we will reap a harvest if we do not give up. 10 Therefore, as we have opportunity, let us do good to all people, especially to those who belong to the family of believers.

- Honoring God with our lives is NEVER pointless. What are we promised?

- When are we most tempted to give up?

1 Peter 5:6-9

6 Humble yourselves, therefore, under God's mighty hand, that he may lift you up in due time. 7 Cast all your anxiety on him because he cares for you. 8 Be self-controlled and alert. Your enemy the devil prowls around like a roaring lion looking for someone to devour. 9 Resist him, standing firm in the faith, because you know that your brothers throughout the world are undergoing the same kind of sufferings.

Hebrews 10:35-36

35 So do not throw away your confidence; it will be richly rewarded. 36 You need to persevere so that when you have done the will of God, you will receive what he has promised.

- What does Peter advise us to cast off?

- What does Hebrews remind us to not throw away?

- Reflect on your recent "trash pile"—what have you been discarding?

- Suffering is universal. What are we advised to do to enable us to thrive?

- What is the requirement to receive what God has promised?

Revelation 21:6-8

[6] *He said to me: "It is done. I am the Alpha and the Omega, the Beginning and the End. To him who is thirsty I will give to drink without cost from the spring of the water of life.* [7] *He who overcomes will inherit all this, and I will be his God and he will be my son.* [8] *But the cowardly, the unbelieving, the vile, the murderers, the sexually immoral, those who practice magic arts, the idolaters and all liars—their place will be in the fiery lake of burning sulfur. This is the second death."*

- What is required to inherit the Kingdom of God?

- Reflect on seasons when you have endured, persevered, and overcome. What lessons have you learned from God's faithfulness?

SOME STORIES ARE SIMPLE:

- LITTLE RED RIDING HOOD
- THE UGLY DUCKLING

DAILY REFLECTIONS

These are daily reviews of the key Bible verses and related others that will help you think about and apply the insights from this session.

DAY 1

Psalm 91:1-2
Psalm of Protection

¹ Whoever dwells in the shelter of the Most High will rest in the shadow of the Almighty. ² I will say of the LORD, "He is my refuge and my fortress, my God, in whom I trust."

Reflection Question:
How do you develop your relationships with family or friends? Think of a few ways you can get to know God and "dwell" in Him.

DAY 2

Proverbs 2:3-6
Knowledge

³ And if you call out for insight and cry aloud for understanding, ⁴ and if you look for it as for silver and search for it as for hidden treasure, ⁵ then you will understand the fear of the LORD and find the knowledge of God. ⁶ For the LORD gives wisdom, and from his mouth come knowledge and understanding.

Reflection Question:
What is required of us to understand the fear of the Lord?

DAY 3

Proverbs 22:4
Wealth, Honor, Life

Humility and the fear of the LORD bring wealth and honor and life.

Reflection Question:
How can you change your focus to cultivate what God requires in order to bring you wealth, honor, and life?

DAY 4

Ecclesiastes 12:13-14

The Whole Duty of Man

13 Now all has been heard; here is the conclusion of the matter: fear God and keep his commandments, for this is the whole duty of man. 14 For God will bring every deed into judgment, including every hidden thing, whether it is good or evil.

Reflection Question:
Take a moment and write down three things you want to be remembered for when you meet Jesus and three things you would like Him to have forgotten.

DAY 5

Psalm 1:1-3

The Fruitful Tree

1 Blessed is the man who does not walk in the counsel of the wicked or stand in the way of sinners or sit in the seat of mockers. 2 But his delight is in the law of the LORD, and on his law he meditates day and night. 3 He is like a tree planted by streams of water, which yields its fruit in season and whose leaf does not wither. Whatever he does prospers.

Reflection Question:
All of us want to be like the fruitful tree, prospering in all we do. What are some steps you can take to align yourself with what God requires?

WEEKLY MEMORY VERSE

HUMILITY AND THE FEAR OF THE LORD BRING WEALTH AND HONOR AND LIFE.

PROVERBS 22:4

WEEK 5

INTRODUCTION

The Second Temple period is a pivotal time in Jewish history. This season begins with the construction of the second temple in Jerusalem by Zerubbabel and extends through the Roman Period when the Temple is destroyed in 70 AD. Herod the Great expanded the Temple Mount and provided a general upgrade to the temple. It was this temple that Jesus visited during His time in Jerusalem.

THE SECOND TEMPLE 91

The Second Temple period is a way of understanding history, marking the end of the exile of the Jewish people from their homeland and the beginning of a new opportunity. For a brief time, about one hundred years, Israel gained independence under the Hasmonean rulers. The coming of Rome signaled a new time in the life of the Jewish people. Our story this week begins with the returning exiles—Ezra and Nehemiah.

IN THE
BEGINNING...

CREATION   ABRAHAM   THE EXODUS   JUDGES   A UNITED MONARCHY   NATION DIVIDED

CREATION

ABRAHAM

THE EXODUS

JUDGES

A UNITED
MONARCHY

NATION
DIVIDED

GETTING STARTED

Begin the session with a question below or brief activity to
become better acquainted with one another.

1 Have you ever been
a part of building
something—a new
home, a church?
Describe the journey.

2 What is the best thing
about coming home
from a trip?

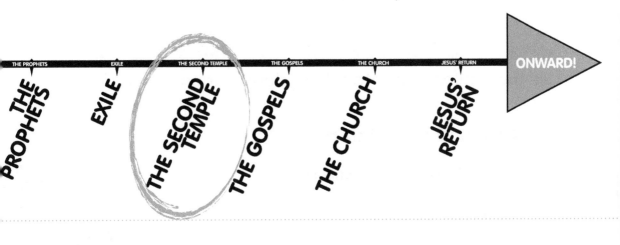

THE PROPHETS · EXILE · THE SECOND TEMPLE · THE GOSPELS · THE CHURCH · JESUS' RETURN · ONWARD!

NEHEMIAH CAME TO THE RESCUE

HE WAS A KING'S CUPBEARER

GOOD?

WELL, THE CHICKEN'S A LITTLE DRY BUT I'M NOT DEAD

HE HEARD NEWS ABOUT THE BROKEN DOWN WALL AROUND JERUSALEM AND THE TEMPLE

WITH YOUR PERMISSION, SIR

CAN I GO REBUILD THE WALL?

YEP

GOOD FOR ONE FREE TRIP OUT OF THE KINGDOM

OUTLINE OF DVD LESSON

Use the outline below to follow along during the DVD.

I. Return and Rebuilding

A. Temple Rebuilt—Zerubbabel

B. Ezra Returns

II. Jerusalem

Nehemiah 1:1-4

¹ The words of Nehemiah . . . ² one of my brothers, came from Judah with some other men, and I questioned them about the Jewish remnant that survived the exile, and also about Jerusalem. . . . ³ They said to me, "Those who survived the exile and are back in the province are in great trouble and disgrace. The wall of Jerusalem is broken down, and its gates have been burned with fire." ⁴ When I heard these things, I sat down and wept. For some days I mourned and fasted and prayed before the God of heaven.

Nehemiah 4:9-14

⁹ But we prayed to our God and posted a guard day and night to meet this threat. ¹⁰ Meanwhile, the people in Judah said, "The strength of the laborers is giving out, and there is so much rubble that we cannot rebuild the wall." ¹¹ Also our enemies said, "Before they know it or see us, we will be right there among them and will kill them and put an end to the work." ¹² Then the Jews who lived near them came and told us ten times over, "Wherever you turn, they will attack us." ¹³ Therefore I stationed some of the people behind the lowest points of the wall at the exposed places, posting them by families, with their swords, spears and bows. ¹⁴ After I looked things over, I stood up and said to the nobles, the officials and the rest of the people, "Don't be afraid of them. Remember the Lord, who is great and awesome, and fight for your brothers, your sons and your daughters, your wives and your homes."

A. Prayed and Stood Guard (v. 9)
James 5:16
The prayer of a righteous man is powerful and effective.

B. Wrestled with Weariness (v. 10)
Psalm 73:2-3
2 But as for me, my feet had almost slipped; I had nearly lost my foothold.
3 For I envied the arrogant when I saw the prosperity of the wicked.

C. Threats (v. 11)
Matthew 4:3
The tempter came to him and said, "If you are the Son of God, tell these stones to become bread."

D. Antagonists (v.12)

E. Attention to Defense (v.13)
Ephesians 6:10-11
10 Finally, be strong in the Lord and in his mighty power. 11 Put on the full armor of God so that you can take your stand against the devil's schemes.

A MIGHTY SOURCE

SECOND TEMPLE:

THE ISRAELITES WERE IN A PERIOD OF CONFUSION AND DARKNESS

MIDDLESBORO KY

WE'VE BEEN RUN OUT OF THE PROMISED LAND, THE TEMPLE'S BEEN DESTROYED, OUR PEOPLE ARE SCATTERED, WE'RE SERVANTS, IT'S DARK, AND WE'RE WEARING SUNGLASSES.

WE'RE JUST LIKE THE ISRAELITES

25

HARROGATE TN

NEHEMIAH CAME TO THE RESCUE

HE WAS A KING'S CUPBEARER

GOOD?

WELL, THE CHICKEN'S A LITTLE DRY BUT I'M NOT DEAD

HE HEARD NEWS ABOUT THE BROKEN DOWN WALL AROUND JERUSALEM AND THE TEMPLE

WITH YOUR PERMISSION, SIR

CAN I GO REBUILD THE WALL?

YEP

GOOD FOR ONE FREE TRIP OUT OF THE KINGDOM

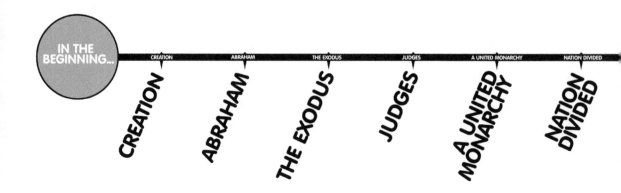

IN THE BEGINNING...

CREATION

ABRAHAM

THE EXODUS

JUDGES

A UNITED MONARCHY

NATION DIVIDED

DISCUSSION

Using the questions that follow, we will review and expand on the teaching we just experienced.

Daniel 9:1-2

¹ In the first year of Darius son of Xerxes (a Mede by descent), who was made ruler over the Babylonian kingdom—² in the first year of his reign, I, Daniel, understood from the Scriptures, according to the word of the LORD given to Jeremiah the prophet, that the desolation of Jerusalem would last seventy years.

1 How did Daniel know it was time for the Exile to end?

2 Peter 1:19-21

¹⁹ And we have the word of the prophets made more certain, and you will do well to pay attention to it, as to a light shining in a dark place, until the day dawns and the morning star rises in your hearts. ²⁰ Above all, you must understand that no prophecy of Scripture came about by the prophet's own interpretation. ²¹ For prophecy never had its origin in the will of man, but men spoke from God as they were carried along by the Holy Spirit.

2 What did Peter reveal as the origin of prophecy?

Ezra 7:8-10

⁸ Ezra arrived in Jerusalem in the fifth month of the seventh year of the king. ⁹ He had begun his journey from Babylon on the first day of the first month, and he arrived in Jerusalem on the first day of the fifth month, for the gracious hand of his God was on him. ¹⁰ For Ezra had devoted himself to the study and observance of the Law of the LORD, and to teaching its decrees and laws in Israel.

3 How long did it take Ezra to travel to Jerusalem from Babylon?

4 What was Ezra's objective in returning?

Nehemiah 1:1-4

[1] *The words of Nehemiah . . .* [2] *Hanani, one of my brothers, came from Judah with some other men, and I questioned them about the Jewish remnant that survived the exile, and also about Jerusalem.* [3] *They said to me, "Those who survived the exile and are back in the province are in great trouble and disgrace. The wall of Jerusalem is broken down, and its gates have been burned with fire."* [4] *When I heard these things, I sat down and wept. For some days I mourned and fasted and prayed before the God of heaven.*

5 What was Nehemiah's response when he heard about the condition of Jerusalem?

Nehemiah 4:1-2

[1] *When Sanballat heard that we were rebuilding the wall, he became angry and was greatly incensed. He ridiculed the Jews,* [2] *and in the presence of his associates and the army of Samaria, he said, "What are those feeble Jews doing? Will they restore their wall? Will they offer sacrifices? Will they finish in a day? Can they bring the stones back to life from those heaps of rubble—burned as they are?"*

6 What was the response of the local citizens when the exiles began to rebuild the city wall of Jerusalem?

APPLICATION

Now it's time to make some personal applications of all we've been thinking about in the last few minutes.

THE WHITEBOARD BIBLE

READ ALOUD

Zerubbabel, Ezra, and Nehemiah were leaders in an initiative to rebuild the temple and restore Jerusalem. They made personal sacrifices, invested a great deal of effort, and risked everything to help God's people have a new beginning. Renewal does not happen in a vacuum. Typically it emerges because someone cares enough about the purposes of God to make an extraordinary effort.

The book of Nehemiah provides a pattern for restoration. We serve a God who redeems and restores. The process will require participation.

Nehemiah 4:9-14

⁹ But we prayed to our God and posted a guard day and night to meet this threat. ¹⁰ Meanwhile, the people in Judah said, "The strength of the laborers is giving out, and there is so much rubble that we cannot rebuild the wall." ¹¹ Also our enemies said, "Before they know it or see us, we will be right there among them and will kill them and put an end to the work." ¹² Then the Jews who lived near them came and told us ten times over, "Wherever you turn, they will attack us." ¹³ Therefore I stationed some of the people behind the lowest points of the wall at the exposed places, posting them by families, with their swords, spears and bows. ¹⁴ After I looked things over, I stood up and said to the nobles, the officials and the rest of the people, "Don't be afraid of them. Remember the Lord, who is great and awesome, and fight for your brothers, your sons and your daughters, your wives and your homes."

7 What challenges did Nehemiah face as they began? How did they respond?

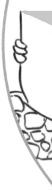

8 Have you experienced opposition when you tried to cooperate with God? Explain.

READ ALOUD

Often we imagine that saying yes to God will eliminate all other obstacles. We frequently respond with surprise and disappointment when our efforts in the name of the Lord meet opposition. The story of the Bible reminds us that God's purposes seldom go unchallenged. We must be prepared physically, spiritually, and emotionally to fulfill God's invitations.

9 What was the general attitude of those with Nehemiah?

10 Nehemiah's response was to arm the workers. Read Ephesians 6:13-17. What weapons do we have at our disposal as we serve the Lord?

11 Nehemiah gave instructions to the people, advising two basic responses: 1) do not be afraid; 2) fight for your families and homes. How do we overcome fear and stand up for our families in this generation?

12 Nehemiah's attitude toward God is key. What did he remind the people of about God?

READ ALOUD
Nehemiah rebuilt the wall around Jerusalem. Without the wall, the inhabitants of the city were unprotected and vulnerable. The Church is a protection for people in our generation. We are assigned with building up the Church to provide hope and protection for our community.

13 We have the privilege of telling our generation about a great and awesome God. How can we share our Jesus-story with others? What responses should be anticipated?

14 Discuss ways to encourage and support one another as you "build up the walls" for our generation.

THINGS WERE LOOKING UP

AND REBUILT THE
WALL IN 52 DAYS

THE PEOPLE REPENTED
AND WORSHIPPED

PRAYER

Close the session in prayer. Share prayer requests with the group, and pray for each other. Close by praying the following prayer together.

Heavenly Father, thank You for the privilege of hearing Your Word. We choose to open our hearts and receive all that You have for us. We say "yes" to You. We want to be cooperative. Forgive our sins, our rebellion, and our idolatry. Apart from You we have no hope, but in You there is mercy and forgiveness. We rejoice in Your faithfulness. May our lives be pleasing in Your sight. In Jesus name, amen.

Prayer requests this week:

GOING DEEPER

This section is designed to do as homework, if you choose, between your Small Group meetings.

Guarding Our Hearts and Lives

Proverbs 4:23
Above all else, guard your heart, for it is the wellspring of life.

- List three or four things you intentionally guard/protect. What types of efforts or resources are involved in the protection?

- In what ways is your heart vulnerable?

- How could you begin to guard your heart more effectively?

Luke 11:21-23
[21] "When a strong man, fully armed, guards his own house, his possessions are safe. [22] But when someone stronger attacks and overpowers him, he takes away the armor in which the man trusted and divides up the spoils. [23] "He who is not with me is against me, and he who does not gather with me, scatters."

Ephesians 6:10-18
[10] Finally, be strong in the LORD and in his mighty power. [11] Put on the full armor of God so that you can take your stand against the devil's schemes. [12] For our struggle is not against flesh and blood, but against the rulers, against the authorities, against the powers of this dark world and against the spiritual forces of evil in the heavenly realms. [13] Therefore put on the full armor of God, so that when the day of evil comes, you may be able to stand your ground, and after you have done everything, to stand. [14] Stand firm then, with the belt of truth buckled around your waist, with the breastplate of righteousness in place, [15] and with your feet fitted with the readiness that comes from the gospel of peace. [16] In addition to all this, take up the shield of faith, with which you can extinguish all the flaming arrows of the evil one. [17] Take the helmet of salvation and the sword of the Spirit, which is the word of God. [18] And pray in the Spirit on all occasions with all kinds of prayers and

requests. With this in mind, be alert and always keep on praying for all the saints.

- What does it mean to be strong in the Lord?

- Luke 11:23 tells us, *"He who is not with me is against me, and he who does not gather with me, scatters."* How are you involved in "gathering with Jesus"?

READ ALOUD
The great struggles in our lives have spiritual origins. The delivery systems may be people or organizations, but our ultimate "wrestling match" is with spiritual forces.

- What do you do to gain spiritual strength?

- Which piece of the spiritual armor is the least comfortable for you?

- How could you expand and strengthen your prayer response?

HE HAD THE PRIEST EZRA REMIND THE PEOPLE OF GOD'S FAITHFULNESS

DAILY REFLECTIONS

These are daily reviews of the key Bible verses and related others that will help you think about and apply the insights from this session.

DAY 1

James 5:16

Prayed & Stood Guard

The prayer of a righteous man is powerful and effective.

Reflection Question:
Do you have an obstacle or threat in your life to which you could apply this powerful tool?

DAY 2

Matthew 11:28

Wrestled with Weariness

"Come to me, all you who are weary and burdened, and I will give you rest."

Reflection Question:
When we get tired and overwhelmed by life's circumstances it is easy to lose sight of where our help comes from. When we face opposition, what does Jesus instruct?

DAY 3

Matthew 4:3-4

Threats

3 The tempter came to him and said, "If you are the Son of God, tell these stones to become bread." 4 Jesus answered, "It is written: 'Man does not live on bread alone, but on every word that comes from the mouth of God.'"

Reflection Question:
After forty days of fasting, Jesus was faced with Satan's threats. What was His response? What can we learn through this experience to use when we are threatened?

DAY 4

Hebrews 12:1-2

Antagonists

[1] *Therefore, since we are surrounded by such a great cloud of witnesses, let us throw off everything that hinders and the sin that so easily entangles, and let us run with perseverance the race marked out for us.* [2] *Let us fix our eyes on Jesus, the author and perfecter of our faith.*

Reflection Question:

What does Scripture tell us to do and remember so that we can stand firm and not lose heart?

DAY 5

Ephesians 6:10-11

Attention to Defense

[10] *Finally, be strong in the Lord and in his mighty power.* [11] *Put on the full armor of God so that you can take your stand against the devil's schemes.*

Reflection Question:

The Lord has given us spiritual armor in order to stand against the devil. What is the full armor of God (vv. 14-18)? What pieces of the armor have you not been using?

WEEKLY MEMORY VERSE

[10] FINALLY, BE STRONG IN THE LORD AND IN HIS MIGHTY POWER. PUT ON THE FULL ARMOR OF GOD SO THAT YOU CAN TAKE YOUR STAND AGAINST THE DEVIL'S SCHEMES.

EPHESIANS 6:10-11

WEEK 6

INTRODUCTION

The Gospels tell us the Jesus-story. The historical setting is important. In Jerusalem, the second temple is one of the wonders of the ancient world. Herod the Great undertook a very ambitious expansion of the temple area. The platform for the temple area is still being used in Jerusalem today. Jesus did not grow up in Jerusalem. He grew up in Nazareth, a small village tucked into the hills of northern Israel. Jesus' ministry began in Galilee, not in the power center of Jerusalem. Jesus established Capernaum, a fishing village,

THE GOSPELS

as His ministry center. The four Gospels help us to understand Jesus of Nazareth as the Christ. The story of Jesus is very much a part of the larger story of the Old Testament. Without the context of all that precedes the Gospels, it is almost impossible to grasp the significance of Jesus.

CREATION   ABRAHAM   THE EXODUS   JUDGES   A UNITED MONARCHY   NATION DIVIDED

CREATION

ABRAHAM

THE EXODUS

JUDGES

A UNITED MONARCHY

NATION DIVIDED

112

THE WHITEBOARD BIBLE

GETTING STARTED

Begin the session with a question below or brief activity to become better acquainted with one another.

1 Where was Jesus born?

2 Which angel informed Mary she had been chosen to give birth to the Son of God?

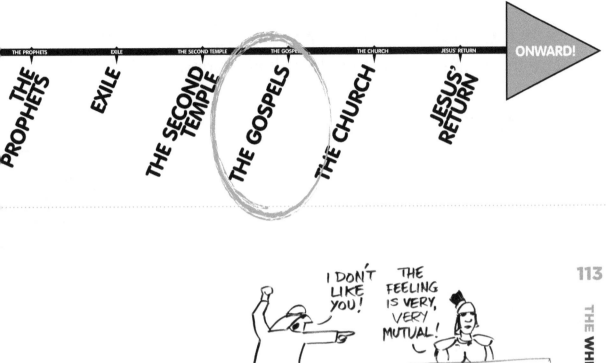

OUTLINE OF DVD LESSON
Use the outline below to follow along during the DVD.

I. Gospels
Matthew
Mark
Luke
John

II. Sects
Pharisees
Sadducees
Essenes
Zealots
Christians

III. Jesus, the Christ

John 14:5-7
5 Thomas said to him, "Lord, we don't know where you are going, so how can we know the way?" 6 Jesus answered, "I am the way and the truth and the life. No one comes to the Father except through me. 7 If you really knew me, you would know my Father as well. From now on, you do know him and have seen him."

A. "With Jesus"—Not Frightened
Luke 13:31-32 (MSG)
31 Just then some Pharisees came up and said, "Run for your life! Herod's on the hunt. He's out to kill you!" 32 Jesus said, "Tell that fox that I've no time for him right now. Today and tomorrow I'm busy clearing out the demons and healing the sick; the third day I'm wrapping things up."

B. "With Jesus"—Not Worried
Matthew 6:31-33
31 "So do not worry, saying, 'What shall we eat?' or 'What shall we drink?' or 'What shall we wear?' 32 For the pagans run after all these things, and your

heavenly Father knows that you need them. ³³ But seek first his kingdom and his righteousness, and all these things will be given to you as well."

C. "With Jesus"—Compassion
Luke 7:12-15

¹² As he approached the town gate, a dead person was being carried out— the only son of his mother, and she was a widow. And a large crowd from the town was with her. ¹³ When the Lord saw her, his heart went out to her and he said, "Don't cry." ¹⁴ Then he went up and touched the coffin, and those carrying it stood still. He said, "Young man, I say to you, get up!" ¹⁵ The dead man sat up and began to talk, and Jesus gave him back to his mother.

Mark 1:40-41

⁴⁰ A man with leprosy came to him and begged him on his knees, "If you are willing, you can make me clean." ⁴¹ Filled with compassion, Jesus reached out his hand and touched the man. "I am willing," he said. "Be clean!"

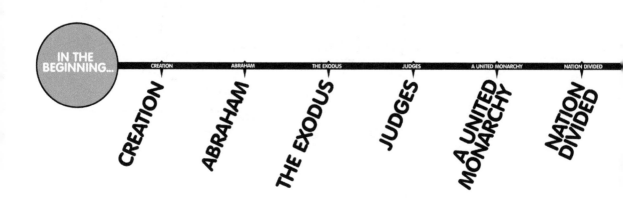

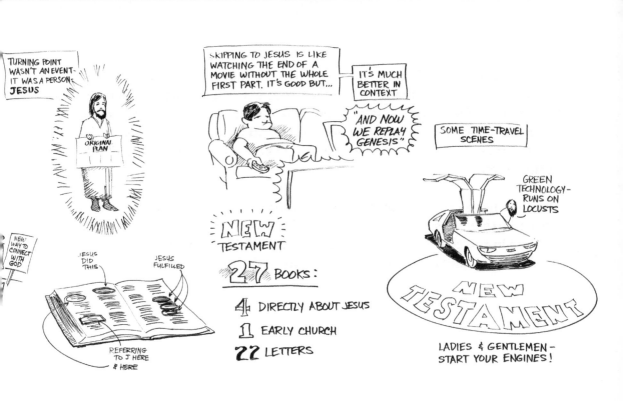

TURNING POINT WASN'T AN EVENT—IT WAS A PERSON: JESUS

ORIGINAL PLAN

SKIPPING TO JESUS IS LIKE WATCHING THE END OF A MOVIE WITHOUT THE WHOLE FIRST PART. IT'S GOOD BUT...

IT'S MUCH BETTER IN CONTEXT

"AND NOW WE REPLAY GENESIS"

SOME TIME-TRAVEL SCENES

GREEN TECHNOLOGY—RUNS ON LOCUSTS

NEW WAY TO CONNECT WITH GOD

JESUS DID THIS

JESUS FULFILLED

REFERRING TO J HERE & HERE

NEW TESTAMENT

27 BOOKS:

4 DIRECTLY ABOUT JESUS

1 EARLY CHURCH

22 LETTERS

NEW TESTAMENT

LADIES & GENTLEMEN—START YOUR ENGINES!

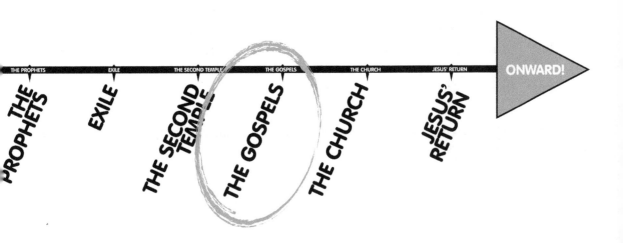

THE PROPHETS   EXILE   THE SECOND TEMPLE   THE GOSPELS   THE CHURCH   JESUS' RETURN   ONWARD!

THE PROPHETS   EXILE   THE SECOND TEMPLE   THE GOSPELS   THE CHURCH   JESUS' RETURN

DISCUSSION

Using the questions that follow, we will review and expand on the teaching we just experienced.

READ ALOUD

Jesus is very much a biblical character like the individuals from the Old Testament. He is a deliverer, a prophet, a priest, a king—someone chosen by God to help His people. Just as many Old Testament leaders were rejected or ignored, Jesus' message was not welcomed by the power brokers in Jerusalem. In this chapter we will compare characters from the Old and New Testaments.

The circumstances of Jesus' birth were supernatural. The circumstances of Isaac's birth were supernatural. Many of the characteristics of Jesus' life can be seen in the characters of the Old Testament. The story of Jesus is very much the completion of what began in Genesis, chapter one.

1 Describe the similarities between Moses' role as deliverer and Jesus' role as deliverer.

Matthew 21:28-32

28 "What do you think? There was a man who had two sons. He went to the first and said, 'Son, go and work today in the vineyard.' 29 'I will not,' he answered, but later he changed his mind and went. 30 Then the father went to the other son and said the same thing. He answered, 'I will, sir,' but he did not go. 31 Which of the two did what his father wanted?" "The first," they answered. Jesus said to them, "I tell you the truth, the tax collectors and the prostitutes are entering the kingdom of God ahead of you. 32 For John came to you to show you the way of righteousness, and you did not believe him, but the tax collectors and the prostitutes did. And even after you saw this, you did not repent and believe him."

2 Elijah called Israel to repentance. How did Jesus challenge the leadership of Israel to change?

3 List three or four miracles from the Old Testament.

John 18:37

"You are a king, then!" said Pilate. Jesus answered, "You are right in saying I am a king. In fact, for this reason I was born, and for this I came into the world, to testify to the truth. Everyone on the side of truth listens to me."

John 19:19-22

[19] Pilate had a notice prepared and fastened to the cross. It read: JESUS OF NAZARETH, KING OF THE JEWS. [20] Many of the Jews read this sign, for the place where Jesus was crucified was near the city, and the sign was written in Aramaic, Latin and Greek. [21] The chief priests of the Jews protested to Pilate, "Do not write 'The King of the Jews,' but that this man claimed to be king of the Jews." [22] Pilate answered, "What I have written, I have written."

4 Jesus said He was a king. Who would you say was the greatest Old Testament king of the Jewish people?

5 What are the implications for our lives when we recognize Jesus as King?

1 Kings 17:1

Now Elijah the Tishbite, from Tishbe in Gilead, said to Ahab, "As the LORD, the God of Israel, lives, whom I serve, there will be neither dew nor rain in the next few years except at my word."

6 Elijah's prayers influenced the pattern of rain. Describe ways Jesus exercised authority over the natural elements.

Ezekiel 3:1-4

¹ *And he said to me, "Son of man, eat what is before you, eat this scroll; then go and speak to the house of Israel." ² So I opened my mouth, and he gave me the scroll to eat. ³ Then he said to me, "Son of man, eat this scroll I am giving you and fill your stomach with it." So I ate it, and it tasted as sweet as honey in my mouth. ⁴ He then said to me: "Son of man, go now to the house of Israel and speak my words to them."*

John 12:49-50

⁴⁹ *"For I did not speak of my own accord, but the Father who sent me commanded me what to say and how to say it. ⁵⁰ I know that his command leads to eternal life. So whatever I say is just what the Father has told me to say."*

7 How is Jesus' assignment similar to Ezekiel's?

READ ALOUD

Jesus is very much an individual of the Old Testament. His life and ministry are an extension of the character of God and the patterns of ministry that we find throughout the Old Testament. Jesus is a prophet, priest, and king.

APPLICATION

Now it's time to make some personal applications of all we've been thinking about in the last few minutes.

Matthew 1:16
And Jacob the father of Joseph, the husband of Mary, of whom was born Jesus, who is called Christ.

Mark 1:1 (KJV)
The beginning of the gospel of Jesus Christ, the Son of God.

Luke 1:30-33
30 But the angel said to her, "Do not be afraid, Mary, you have found favor with God. 31 You will be with child and give birth to a son, and you are to give him the name Jesus. 32 He will be great and will be called the Son of the Most High. The Lord God will give him the throne of his father David, 33 and he will reign over the house of Jacob forever; his kingdom will never end."

John 1:1-14
1 In the beginning was the Word, and the Word was with God, and the Word was God. 2 He was with God in the beginning. 3 Through him all things were made; without him nothing was made that has been made. 4 In him was life, and that life was the light of men. 5 The light shines in the darkness, but the darkness has not understood it. 11 He came to that which was his own, but his own did not receive him. 12 Yet to all who received him, to those who believed in his name, he gave the right to become children of God— 13 children born not of natural descent, nor of human decision or a husband's will, but born of God. 14 The Word became flesh and made his dwelling among us. We have seen his glory, the glory of the One and Only, who came from the Father, full of grace and truth.

8 List the descriptions attributed to Jesus in each of the Gospel introductions.

READ ALOUD

Jesus is the fulfillment of what the story of Scripture has pointed to. The law, the prophets, and the insights into the character of God were fulfilled in Jesus. The message of the New Testament is very much a part of the events of the Old Testament. The author of Hebrews makes this point directly in chapter one.

> Hebrews 1:1-4
>
> *¹ In the past God spoke to our forefathers through the prophets at many times and in various ways, ² but in these last days he has spoken to us by his Son, whom he appointed heir of all things, and through whom he made the universe. ³ The Son is the radiance of God's glory and the exact representation of his being, sustaining all things by his powerful word. After he had provided purification for sins, he sat down at the right hand of the Majesty in heaven. ⁴ So he became as much superior to the angels as the name he has inherited is superior to theirs.*

9 This passage in Hebrews provides insight into seven specific revelations regarding Jesus. List them.

1. heir of all things
2. through whom God made the universe
3. radiance of God's glory
4.
5.
6.
7.

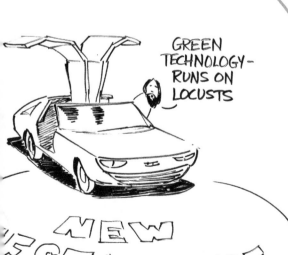

SOME TIME-TRAVEL SCENES

GREEN TECHNOLOGY — RUNS ON LOCUSTS

NEW TESTAMENT

READ ALOUD

The Gospels present a compelling picture of Jesus. The first disciples came to understand that being with Jesus changed every aspect of their lives. Even after Jesus ascended back to heaven, the power of that relationship changed the way the disciples faced life. In a similar way, we are invited to a relationship with Jesus. Christ in us changes how we negotiate life.

Luke 13:31-32 (MSG)
31 Just then some Pharisees came up and said, "Run for your life! Herod's on the hunt. He's out to kill you!" 32 Jesus said, "Tell that fox that I've no time for him right now. Today and tomorrow I'm busy clearing out the demons and healing the sick; the third day I'm wrapping things up."

Luke 8:52-55
52 Meanwhile, all the people were wailing and mourning for her. "Stop wailing," Jesus said. "She is not dead but asleep." 53 They laughed at him, knowing that she was dead. 54 But he took her by the hand and said, "My child, get up!" 55 Her spirit returned, and at once she stood up. Then Jesus told them to give her something to eat.

124

10 Jesus confronted life fearlessly. He endured threats and even faced death. Discuss places where fear encroaches on our lives and how we can learn to put our trust in Jesus to gain new freedoms.

Matthew 6:31-33
31 "So do not worry, saying, 'What shall we eat?' or 'What shall we drink?' or 'What shall we wear?' 32 For the pagans run after all these things, and your heavenly Father knows that you need them. 33 But seek first his kingdom and his righteousness, and all these things will be given to you as well."

11 Jesus' life was not characterized by worry. What does Jesus encourage us to make our first priority?

12 If Jesus directs us not to worry, what is worry?

13 What does Jesus tell us God will give us?

THE WHITEBOARD BIBLE

READ ALOUD

A relationship with Jesus transforms our lives. Jesus gives us a God-perspective that brings a whole new set of possibilities to our lives. The decision to be a Christ-follower is not about joining a religion or a church. To acknowledge Jesus as the Christ and choose Him as Lord is a very personal and dynamic decision. Every day becomes a remarkable adventure as we learn about the character, grace, and majesty of our Lord.

14 Take a few moments and discuss ways you have come to trust the grace and goodness of Jesus in your lives. How do these experiences reflect the character of God that we have been reading about in the Old Testament?

15 This concludes the Small Group teaching for Volume 2. Take a minute and discuss your group's plans for Volume 3.

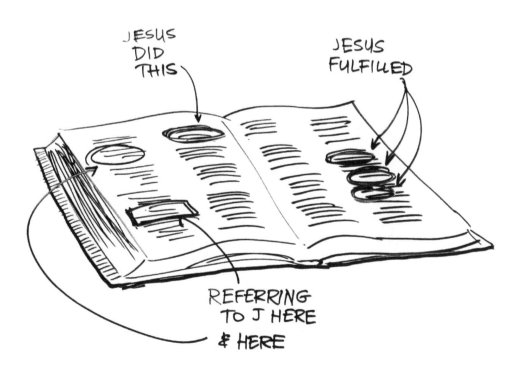

JESUS DID THIS

JESUS FULFILLED

REFERRING TO J HERE & HERE

PRAYER

Close the session in prayer. Share prayer requests with the group, and pray for each other. Close by praying the following prayer together.

 Heavenly Father, open our eyes to see Jesus. Holy Spirit, illumine our minds that we might understand the wonder of what Jesus accomplished for us. Forgive us for our reluctance to trust and be obedient. May we have new boldness to be advocates for Jesus of Nazareth; may our lives bring glory and honor to Him. In Jesus' name, amen.

Prayer requests this week:

_____

_____

_____

_____

_____

_____

_____

GOING DEEPER

This section is designed to do as homework, if you choose, between your Small Group meetings.

···

Listening to Jesus

John 10:1-7

[1] *"I tell you the truth, the man who does not enter the sheep pen by the gate, but climbs in by some other way, is a thief and a robber.* [2] *The man who enters by the gate is the shepherd of his sheep.* [3] *The watchman opens the gate for him, and the sheep listen to his voice. He calls his own sheep by name and leads them out.* [4] *When he has brought out all his own, he goes on ahead of them, and his sheep follow him because they know his voice.* [5] *But they will never follow a stranger; in fact, they will run away from him because they do not recognize a stranger's voice."* [6] *Jesus used this figure of speech, but they did not understand what he was telling them.* [7] *Therefore Jesus said again, "I tell you the truth, I am the gate for the sheep."*

- The way into the Kingdom of God is a person. What is His name?

- What is a primary characteristic of those who follow the Shepherd?

Matthew 6:25-34

[25] *"Therefore I tell you, do not worry about your life, what you will eat or drink; or about your body, what you will wear. Is not life more important than food, and the body more important than clothes?* [26] *Look at the birds of the air; they do not sow or reap or store away in barns, and yet your heavenly Father feeds them. Are you not much more valuable than they?* [27] *Who of you by worrying can add a single hour to his life?* [28] *"And why do you worry about clothes? See how the lilies of the field grow. They do not labor or spin.* [29] *Yet I tell you that not even Solomon in all his splendor was dressed like one of these.* [30] *If that is how God clothes the grass of the field, which is here today and tomorrow is thrown into the fire, will he not much more clothe you, O you of little faith?* [31] *So do not worry, saying, 'What shall we eat?' or 'What shall we drink?' or 'What shall we wear?'* [32] *For the pagans run after all these things, and your heavenly Father knows that you need them.* [33] *But seek first his kingdom and his righteousness, and all these things will be given to you as well.* [34] *Therefore do not worry about tomorrow, for tomorrow will worry about itself. Each day has enough trouble of its own."*

- What does Jesus tell us not to do?

- What is the lesson from the birds?

- What is the lesson from the lilies?

- What should be our first priority?

- What things fill your heart and mind with anxiety? How can you begin to let trust grow in these areas?

DAILY REFLECTIONS

These are daily reviews of the key Bible verses and related others that will help you think about and apply the insights from this session.

DAY 1

Galatians 3:14

My Redemption

He redeemed us in order that the blessing given to Abraham might come to the Gentiles through Christ Jesus, so that by faith we might receive the promise of the Spirit.

Reflection Question:
How can we welcome the Holy Spirit?

DAY 2

2 Corinthians 5:17-18

New Creation

[17] Therefore, if anyone is in Christ, he is a new creation; the old has gone, the new has come! [18] All this is from God, who reconciled us to himself through Christ and gave us the ministry of reconciliation.

Reflection Question:
Why has God given us this great gift through Christ?

DAY 3

Philippians 4:13

Through Christ

I can do everything through him who gives me strength.

Reflection Question:
Where in your life do you feel the weakest? Can you believe Christ can and will give you strength to have victory in this area?

DAY 4

2 Timothy 1:7

Power

For God did not give us a spirit of timidity, but a spirit of power, of love and of self-discipline.

Reflection Question:
Where could power, love and self-discipline change your circumstances?

_____

_____

_____

_____

_____

_____

_____

DAY 5

Matthew 6:30

Provision

"If that is how God clothes the grass of the field, which is here today and tomorrow is thrown into the fire, will he not much more clothe you— O you of little faith?"

Reflection Question:
What things do you worry about? List them and ask God to give you faith to believe He will give you what you need.

_____

_____

_____

_____

_____

_____

WEEKLY MEMORY VERSE

JESUS SAID TO HER, "I AM THE RESURRECTION AND THE LIFE. HE WHO BELIEVES IN ME WILL LIVE, EVEN THOUGH HE DIES."

JOHN 11:25

APPENDIX

FREQUENTLY ASKED QUESTIONS

What do we do on the first night of our group?
Like all fun things in life–have a party! A "get to know you" coffee, dinner, or dessert is a great way to launch a new study. You may want to review the Small Group Agreement page and share the names of a few friends you can invite to join you. But most important, have fun before your study time begins.

Where do we find new members for our group?
We encourage you to pray with your group and then brainstorm a list of people from work, church, your neighborhood, your children's school, family, the gym, and so forth. Then have each group member invite several of the people on his or her list.

No matter how you find participants, it's vital that you stay on the lookout for new people to join your group. All groups tend to go through healthy attrition–the result of moves, releasing new leaders, ministry opportunities, and so forth–and if the group gets too small, it could be at risk of shutting down. If you and your group stay open, you'll be amazed at the people God sends your way. The next person just might become a friend for life. You never know!

How long will this group meet?
It's totally up to the group–once you come to the end of this six-week study. Most groups meet weekly for at least their first six weeks, but every other week can work as well.

At the end of this study, each group member may decide if he or she wants to continue on for another six-week study. Some groups launch relationships for years to come, and others are stepping-stones into another group experience. Either way, enjoy the journey.

What if this group is not working for us?

You're not alone! This could be the result of a personality conflict, life stage difference, geographical distance, level of spiritual maturity, or any number of things. Relax. Pray for God's direction, and at the end of this six-week study, decide whether to continue with this group or find another. You don't buy the first car you look at or marry the first person you date, and the same goes with a group. Don't bail out before the six weeks are up–God might have something to teach you. Also, don't run from conflict or prejudge people before you have given them a chance. God is still working in you too!

How do we handle the child care needs in our group?

We suggest that you empower the group to openly brainstorm solutions. You may try one option that works for a while and then adjust over time. Our favorite approach is for adults to meet in the living room and share the cost of a babysitter (or two) who can be with the kids in a different part of the house. In this way, parents don't have to be away from their children all evening when their children are too young to be left at home. A second option is to use one home for the kids and a second home (close by or a phone call away) for the adults. A third idea is to rotate the responsibility of providing a lesson or care for the children either in the same home or in another home nearby. This can be an incredible blessing for kids. Finally, the most common idea is to decide that you need to have a night to invest in your spiritual lives and to make your own arrangements for child care. No matter what decision the group makes, the best approach is to dialogue openly about both the problem and the solution.

SMALL GROUP AGREEMENT

Our Expectations:

To provide a predictable environment where participants experience authentic community and spiritual growth.

Group Attendance	We would like for everyone to make it a priority to attend each week.
Safe Environment	To help create a safe place where people can be heard and feel loved.
Respect Differences	To be gentle and gracious to fellow group members with different spiritual maturity, personal opinions, temperaments, or "imperfections." We are all works in progress.
Confidentiality	To keep anything that is shared strictly confidential and within the group, and to avoid sharing improper information about those outside the group.
Encouragement for Growth	To be not just takers but givers of life. We want to spiritually multiply our lives by serving others with our God-given gifts.
Shared Ownership	To remember that every member is a minister and to ensure that each attender will share a small team role or responsibility over time (i.e. bringing food or closing in prayer).
Rotating Hosts/ Leaders and Homes	To encourage different people to host the group in their homes, and to rotate the responsibility of facilitating each meeting (see the Small Group Calendar).

Our Times Together:

- Refreshments _____
- Childcare _____
- When we will meet (day of week) _____
- Where we will meet (place) _____
- We will begin at (time) _____ and end at _____
- We will do our best to have some or all of us attend a worship service together.

  Our primary worship service time will be _____

SMALL GROUP CALENDAR

Planning and calendaring can help ensure the greatest participation at every meeting. Be sure to include birthdays, socials, church events, holidays, and projects.

DATE	LESSON	HOST HOME	REFRESHMENTS	LEADER
MONDAY JAN 15	1	BILL	JOE	BILL

MEMORY VERSES

Week 1
⁶ Do not be anxious about anything, but in everything, by prayer and petition, with thanksgiving, present your requests to God. ⁷ And the peace of God, which transcends all understanding, will guard your hearts and your minds in Christ Jesus.
Philippians 4:6-7

Week 2
*But the plans of the L*ORD *stand firm forever, the purposes of his heart through all generations.*
Psalm 33:11

Week 3
Pray for the peace of Jerusalem: "May those who love you be secure."
Psalm 122:6

Week 4
*Humility and the fear of the L*ORD *bring wealth and honor and life.*
Proverbs 22:4

Week 5
¹⁰ Finally, be strong in the Lord and in his mighty power. ¹¹ Put on the full armor of God so that you can take your stand against the devil's schemes.
Ephesians 6:10-11

Week 6
Jesus said to her, "I am the resurrection and the life. He who believes in me will live, even though he dies."
John 11:25

PRAYER AND PRAISE REPORT

	Prayer Requests	Praise Reports
Week 1		
Week 2		
Week 3		
Week 4		
Week 5		
Week 6		

NOTES

One-Year Bible Reading Plan

Week 1
- ☐ Gen. 1-3
- ☐ Gen. 4-7
- ☐ Gen. 8-11
- ☐ Gen. 12-15
- ☐ Gen. 16-18
- ☐ Gen. 19-21
- ☐ Gen. 22-24

Week 2
- ☐ Gen. 25-26
- ☐ Gen. 27-29
- ☐ Gen. 30-31
- ☐ Gen. 32-34
- ☐ Gen. 35-37
- ☐ Gen. 38-40
- ☐ Gen. 41-42

Week 3
- ☐ Gen. 43-45
- ☐ Gen. 46-47
- ☐ Gen. 48-50
- ☐ Exod. 1-3
- ☐ Exod. 4-6
- ☐ Exod. 7-9
- ☐ Exod. 10-12

Week 4
- ☐ Exod. 13-15
- ☐ Exod. 16-18
- ☐ Exod. 19-21
- ☐ Exod. 22-24
- ☐ Exod. 25-27
- ☐ Exod. 28-29
- ☐ Exod. 30-32

Week 5
- ☐ Exod. 33-35
- ☐ Exod. 36-38
- ☐ Exod. 39-40
- ☐ Lev. 1-4
- ☐ Lev. 5-7
- ☐ Lev. 8-10
- ☐ Lev. 11-13

Week 6
- ☐ Lev. 14-15
- ☐ Lev. 16-17
- ☐ Lev. 18-19
- ☐ Lev. 20-21
- ☐ Lev. 22-23
- ☐ Lev. 24-25
- ☐ Lev. 26-27

Week 7
- ☐ Num. 1-4
- ☐ Num. 5-6
- ☐ Num. 7
- ☐ Num. 8-10
- ☐ Num. 11-13
- ☐ Num. 14-15
- ☐ Num. 16-17

Week 8
- ☐ Num. 18-20
- ☐ Num. 21-22
- ☐ Num. 23-25
- ☐ Num. 26-27
- ☐ Num. 28-30
- ☐ Num. 31-33
- ☐ Num. 34-36

Week 9
- ☐ Deut. 1
- ☐ Deut. 2
- ☐ Deut. 3-4
- ☐ Deut. 5-7
- ☐ Deut. 8-10
- ☐ Deut. 11-13
- ☐ Deut. 14-16

Week 10
- ☐ Deut. 17-19
- ☐ Deut. 20-22
- ☐ Deut. 23-25
- ☐ Deut. 26-27
- ☐ Deut. 28-30
- ☐ Deut. 31-32
- ☐ Deut. 33-34

Week 11
- ☐ Josh. 1-4
- ☐ Josh. 5-8
- ☐ Josh. 9-12
- ☐ Josh. 13-16
- ☐ Josh. 17-20
- ☐ Josh. 21-22
- ☐ Josh. 23-24

Week 12
- ☐ Judg. 1-4
- ☐ Judg. 5-7
- ☐ Judg. 8-10
- ☐ Judg. 11-14
- ☐ Judg. 15-18
- ☐ Judg. 19-21
- ☐ Ruth

Week 13
- ☐ 1 Sam. 1-4
- ☐ 1 Sam. 5-10
- ☐ 1 Sam. 11-14
- ☐ 1 Sam. 15-17
- ☐ 1 Sam. 18-21
- ☐ 1 Sam. 22-25
- ☐ 1 Sam. 26-31

Week 14
- ☐ 2 Sam. 1-4
- ☐ 2 Sam. 5-8
- ☐ 2 Sam. 9-12
- ☐ 2 Sam. 13-15
- ☐ 2 Sam. 16-18
- ☐ 2 Sam. 19-21
- ☐ 2 Sam. 22-24

Week 15
- ☐ 1 Kgs. 1-3
- ☐ 1 Kgs. 4-6
- ☐ 1 Kgs. 7-8
- ☐ 1 Kgs. 9-11
- ☐ 1 Kgs. 12-15
- ☐ 1 Kgs. 16-19
- ☐ 1 Kgs. 20-22

Week 16
- ☐ 2 Kgs. 1-4
- ☐ 2 Kgs. 5-8
- ☐ 2 Kgs. 9-11
- ☐ 2 Kgs. 12-15
- ☐ 2 Kgs. 16-18
- ☐ 2 Kgs. 19-22
- ☐ 2 Kgs. 23-25

Week 17
- ☐ 1 Chron. 1-2
- ☐ 1 Chron. 3-5
- ☐ 1 Chron. 6-7
- ☐ 1 Chron. 8-10
- ☐ 1 Chron. 11-17
- ☐ 1 Chron. 18-23
- ☐ 1 Chron. 24-26

Week 18
- ☐ 1 Chron. 27-29
- ☐ 2 Chron. 1-5
- ☐ 2 Chron. 6-9
- ☐ 2 Chron. 10-15
- ☐ 2 Chron. 16-20
- ☐ 2 Chron. 21-25
- ☐ 2 Chron. 26-29

Week 19
- ☐ 2 Chron. 30-32
- ☐ 2 Chron. 33-36
- ☐ Ezra 1-3
- ☐ Ezra 4-7
- ☐ Ezra 8-10
- ☐ Neh. 1-5
- ☐ Neh. 6-7

Week 20
- ☐ Neh. 8-10
- ☐ Neh. 11-13
- ☐ Est. 1-5
- ☐ Est. 6-10
- ☐ Job 1-5
- ☐ Job 6-9
- ☐ Job 10-13

Week 21
- ☐ Job 14-18
- ☐ Job 19-22
- ☐ Job 23-28
- ☐ Job 29-32
- ☐ Job 33-36
- ☐ Job 37-39
- ☐ Job 40-42

Week 22
- ☐ Ps. 1-9
- ☐ Ps. 10-17
- ☐ Ps. 18
- ☐ Ps. 19-22
- ☐ Ps. 23-29
- ☐ Ps. 30-34
- ☐ Ps. 35-39

Week 23
- ☐ Ps. 40-46
- ☐ Ps. 47-54
- ☐ Ps. 55-61
- ☐ Ps. 62-68
- ☐ Ps. 69-73
- ☐ Ps. 74-77
- ☐ Ps. 78-80

Week 24
- ☐ Ps. 81-87
- ☐ Ps. 88-91
- ☐ Ps. 92-100
- ☐ Ps. 101-104
- ☐ Ps. 105-106
- ☐ Ps. 107-110
- ☐ Ps. 111-118

Week 25
- ☐ Ps. 119:1-88
- ☐ Ps. 119:89-176
- ☐ Ps. 120-125
- ☐ Ps. 126-132
- ☐ Ps. 133-139
- ☐ Ps. 140-145
- ☐ Ps. 146-150

Week 26
- ☐ Prov. 1-3
- ☐ Prov. 4-6
- ☐ Prov. 7-10
- ☐ Prov. 11-14
- ☐ Prov. 15-17
- ☐ Prov. 18-20
- ☐ Prov. 21-23

Week 27
- ☐ Prov. 24-26
- ☐ Prov. 27-29
- ☐ Prov. 30-31
- ☐ Eccles. 1-4
- ☐ Eccles. 5-8
- ☐ Eccles. 9-12
- ☐ Song

Week 28
- ☐ Isa. 1-4
- ☐ Isa. 5-8
- ☐ Isa. 9-13
- ☐ Isa. 14-19
- ☐ Isa. 20-24
- ☐ Isa. 25-29
- ☐ Isa. 30-33

Week 29
- ☐ Isa. 34-37
- ☐ Isa. 38-41
- ☐ Isa. 42-45
- ☐ Isa. 46-51
- ☐ Isa. 52-57
- ☐ Isa. 58-61
- ☐ Isa. 62-66

Week 30
- ☐ Jer. 1-4
- ☐ Jer. 5-9
- ☐ Jer. 10-13
- ☐ Jer. 14-17
- ☐ Jer. 18-22
- ☐ Jer. 23-25
- ☐ Jer. 26-29

Week 31
- ☐ Jer. 30-31
- ☐ Jer. 32-34
- ☐ Jer. 35-37
- ☐ Jer. 38-41
- ☐ Jer. 42-45
- ☐ Jer. 46-48
- ☐ Jer. 49-52

Week 32
- ☐ Lam. 1-2
- ☐ Lam. 3-5
- ☐ Ezek. 1-2
- ☐ Ezek. 3-5
- ☐ Ezek. 6-8
- ☐ Ezek. 9-12
- ☐ Ezek. 13-15

Week 33
- ☐ Ezek. 16-17
- ☐ Ezek. 18-20
- ☐ Ezek. 21-22
- ☐ Ezek. 23-24
- ☐ Ezek. 25-27
- ☐ Ezek. 28-30
- ☐ Ezek. 31-33

Week 34
- ☐ Ezek. 34-36
- ☐ Ezek. 37-39
- ☐ Ezek. 40-42
- ☐ Ezek. 43-45
- ☐ Ezek. 46-48
- ☐ Dan. 1-3
- ☐ Dan. 4-6

Week 35
- ☐ Dan. 7-9
- ☐ Dan. 10-12
- ☐ Hos. 1-7
- ☐ Hos. 8-14
- ☐ Joel
- ☐ Amos 1-5
- ☐ Amos 6-9

Week 36
- ☐ Obad.-Jon.
- ☐ Mic.-Nah.
- ☐ Hab.-Zeph.
- ☐ Hag.
- ☐ Zech. 1-7
- ☐ Zech. 8-14
- ☐ Mal.

Week 37
- ☐ Matt. 1-2
- ☐ Matt. 3-4
- ☐ Matt. 5-6
- ☐ Matt. 7-8
- ☐ Matt. 9-10
- ☐ Matt. 11-12
- ☐ Matt. 13-14

Week 38
- ☐ Matt. 15-17
- ☐ Matt. 18-19
- ☐ Matt. 20-21
- ☐ Matt. 22-23
- ☐ Matt. 24-25
- ☐ Matt. 26
- ☐ Matt. 27-28

Week 39
- ☐ Mark 1-3
- ☐ Mark 4-5
- ☐ Mark 6-7
- ☐ Mark 8-9
- ☐ Mark 10-11
- ☐ Mark 12-14
- ☐ Mark 15-16

Week 40
- ☐ Luke 1
- ☐ Luke 2
- ☐ Luke 3
- ☐ Luke 4-5
- ☐ Luke 6-7
- ☐ Luke 8-9
- ☐ Luke 10-11

Week 41
- ☐ Luke 12-13
- ☐ Luke 14-15
- ☐ Luke 16
- ☐ Luke 17-18
- ☐ Luke 19-20
- ☐ Luke 21-22
- ☐ Luke 23-24

Week 42
- ☐ John 1-3
- ☐ John 4-7
- ☐ John 8-10
- ☐ John 11-13
- ☐ John 14-17
- ☐ John 18-19
- ☐ John 20-21

Week 43
- ☐ Acts 1-2
- ☐ Acts 3
- ☐ Acts 4-6
- ☐ Acts 7-8
- ☐ Acts 9-10
- ☐ Acts 11-13
- ☐ Acts 14-15

Week 44
- ☐ Acts 16-17
- ☐ Acts 18-20
- ☐ Acts 21-23
- ☐ Acts 24-26
- ☐ Acts 27-28
- ☐ Rom. 1-3
- ☐ Rom. 4-7

Week 45
- ☐ Rom. 8-10
- ☐ Rom. 11-13
- ☐ Rom. 14-16
- ☐ 1 Cor. 1-4
- ☐ 1 Cor. 5-8
- ☐ 1 Cor. 9-12
- ☐ 1 Cor. 13-16

Week 46
- [ ] 2 Cor. 1-3
- [ ] 2 Cor. 4-8
- [ ] 2 Cor. 9-11
- [ ] 2 Cor. 12-13
- [ ] Gal. 1-2
- [ ] Gal. 3-4
- [ ] Gal. 5-6

Week 47
- [ ] Eph.
- [ ] Phil.
- [ ] Col.
- [ ] 1 Thess.
- [ ] 2 Thess.
- [ ] 1 Tim.
- [ ] 2 Tim.

Week 48
- [ ] Titus - Philem.
- [ ] Heb. 1-6
- [ ] Heb. 7-10
- [ ] Heb. 11-13
- [ ] Jas.
- [ ] 1 Pet.
- [ ] 2 Pet.

Week 49
- [ ] 1 Jn. - 2 Jn.
- [ ] 3 Jn. - Jude
- [ ] Rev. 1-4
- [ ] Rev. 5-9
- [ ] Rev. 10-14
- [ ] Rev. 15-18
- [ ] Rev. 19-22

Finished! (good job)

NEW ME

SMALL GROUP LEADERS

HOSTING AN OPEN HOUSE

If you're starting a new group, try planning an "open house" before your first formal group meeting. Even if you only have two to four core members, it's a great way to break the ice and to consider prayerfully who else might be open to joining you over the next few weeks. You can also use this kick-off meeting to hand out study guides, collect contact information for each person, ask for each person's birthday so you can later celebrate with them, spend some time getting to know each other, and briefly pray for each other.

A simple meal or good desserts always make a kick-off meeting more fun. After people introduce themselves and share how they ended up being at the meeting (you can play a game to see who has the wildest story!), have everyone respond to a few icebreaker questions: "What is your favorite family vacation?" or "What is one thing you love about your church/our community?" or "What are three things about your life growing up that most people here don't know?" Next, ask everyone to tell what he or she hopes to get out of the study. You might want to review the Small Group Agreement and talk about each person's expectations and priorities.

Finally, set an empty chair in the center of your group and explain that it represents someone who would enjoy or benefit from this group but who isn't here yet. Ask people to pray about whom they could invite to join the group over the next few weeks. Hand out postcards and have everyone write an invitation or two. Don't worry about ending up with too many people; you can always have one discussion circle in the living room and another in the dining room after you watch the lesson. Each group could then report prayer requests and progress at the end of the session.

You can skip this kick-off meeting if your time is limited, but you'll experience a huge benefit if you take the time to connect with each other in this way.

LEADING FOR THE FIRST TIME

- **Sweaty palms are a healthy sign.** The Bible says God is gracious to the humble. Remember who is in control; if you feel inadequate, that is probably a good sign. Those who are soft in heart (and sweaty palmed) are those whom God is sure to speak through.

- **Seek support.** Ask your leader, co-leader, or close friend to pray for you and prepare with you before the session. Walking through the study will help you anticipate potentially difficult questions and discussion topics.

- **Bring your uniqueness to the study.** Lean into who you are and how God wants you to uniquely lead the study.

- **Prepare.** Go through the lesson once before everyone arrives. Take time to listen to the teaching segment (DVD) and choose the questions you want to be sure to discuss.

- **Ask for feedback so you can grow.** Perhaps in an email or on cards handed out at the study, have everyone write down three things you did well and one thing you could improve on.

- **Share with your group what God is doing in your heart.** God is searching for those whose hearts are fully His. Share your trials and victories. We promise that people will relate.

- **One final challenge:** Before your first opportunity to lead, look up each of the five passages listed below. Read each one as a devotional exercise to help equip yourself with a shepherd's heart. Trust us on this one. If you do this, you will be more than ready for your first meeting.

Matthew 9:36
1 Peter 5:2-4
Psalm 23
Ezekiel 34:11-16
1 Thessalonians 2:7-8, 11-12

LEADERSHIP TRAINING 101

Congratulations! You have responded to the call to help shepherd Jesus' flock. There are few other tasks in the family of God that surpass the contribution you will be making. As you prepare to lead, whether it is one session or the entire series, here are a few thoughts to keep in mind. We encourage you to read these and review them with each new discussion leader before he or she leads.

1 **Ask God for help.** Pray right now for God to help you build a healthy group. If you can enlist a co-leader you will find your experience to be much richer.

2 **Just be yourself.** Use your unique gifts and temperament. Don't try to do things exactly like another leader; do them in a way that fits you!

3 **Prepare for your meeting ahead of time.** Review the session and the leader's notes, and write down your responses to each question. Pay special attention to exercises that ask group members to do something other than engage in discussion. Review "Outline for Each Session" so you'll remember the purpose of each section in the study.

4 **Pray for your group members by name.** Before you begin your session, go around the room in your mind and pray for each member by name. You may want to review the prayer list at least once a week. Ask God to use your time together to touch the heart of every person uniquely. Expect God to lead you to whomever He wants you to encourage or challenge in a special way. If you listen, God will surely lead!

5 **When you ask a question, be patient.** Someone will eventually respond. Sometimes people need a moment or two of silence to think about the question; and if silence doesn't bother you, it won't bother anyone else. After someone responds, affirm the response with a simple "thanks" or "good point." Then ask, "How about somebody else?" or "Would someone who hasn't shared like to add anything?" Be sensitive to new people or reluctant members who aren't ready to say, pray, or do anything. If you give them a safe setting, they will blossom over time.

6 **Provide transitions between questions.** When guiding the discussion, use the "READ ALOUD" paragraphs as transitions into the questions. Ask the group if anyone would like to read the paragraph. Don't call on anyone, but ask for a volunteer, and then be patient until someone begins. Be sure to thank the person who reads aloud. These paragraphs can also be used for a more rich discussion if your group wants to expand on what was just read.

NOTES

PASTOR ALLEN JACKSON

Allen Jackson is passionate about helping people become more fully devoted followers of Jesus Christ who respond to Godís invitations for their life.

He has served World Outreach Church since 1981, becoming senior pastor in 1989. Under his leadership, WOC has grown to a congregation of over 15,000 through outreach activities, community events and worship services designed to share the Gospel.

Through Allen Jackson Ministries, his messages reach people across the globe ó through television, radio, Sirius XM, and online streaming. His teachings are also available in published books and other resources. Jackson has spoken at pastorsí conferences in the U.S. and abroad, and has been a featured speaker during Jerusalemís Feast of Tabernacles celebration for the Vision for Israel organization and the International Christian Embassy- Jerusalem. Allen Jackson Ministries coaches pastors around the world, writing and publishing small-group curriculum used in states across the US, as well as Israel, Guatemala, the Philippines, Bermuda, Mexico, the United Kingdom, and South Africa.

With degrees from Oral Roberts University and Vanderbilt University, and additional studies at Gordon-Conwell Theological Seminary and Hebrew University of Jerusalem, Jackson is uniquely equipped to help people develop a love and understanding of Godís Word.

Pastor Jacksonís wife, Kathy, is an active participant in ministry at World Outreach Church.

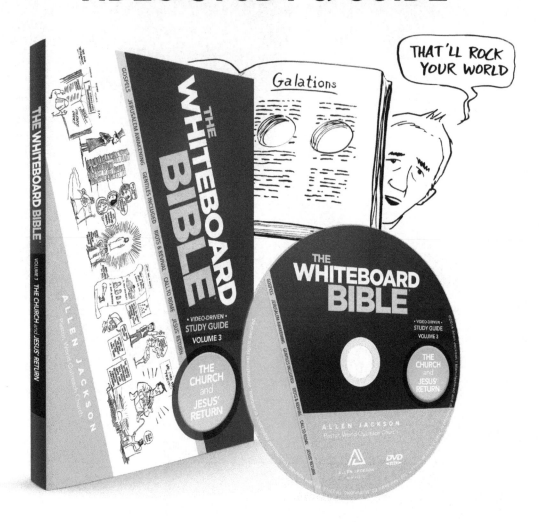

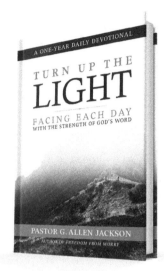
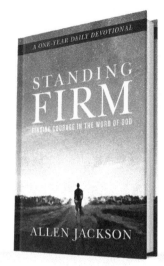
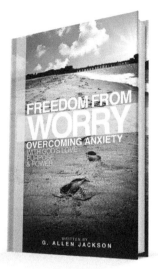

For more from Allen Jackson—including sermons, books, and small group materials—visit:

allenjackson.com